THE PRIMAL METHOD

THE PRIMAL METHOD

A Book for Emerging Men

GREGORY KOUFACOS

Book design by Gray Dog Press and Kevin Breen
Cover image by Junriel Boquecosa

ISBN: 978-1-7360127-0-3
Cataloging-in-Publication Data is available upon request

Manufactured in the United States of America

Production by Gray Dog Press
www.graydogpress.com

Published by
Latah Books, Spokane, Washington
www.latahbooks.com

The author may be contacted at www.theprimalmethod.org

For CG,
To the memory of the world you helped create.
To the memory that is your Soul's to take!

and

For Corinna,
I love you.

Your beloved son — send him on a journey.
可愛い子には旅をさせよ
—Japanese proverb

Contents

Part Two: My Primal Story

Introduction

People in my profession have known something the general public is only now starting to recognize: we are facing an epidemic with our young men. Electronic and chemical addictions, mental breakdowns, overall apathy and listlessness, and lives ending before they have even had a chance to begin. We are losing our young men.

Here is our guy. . . .

He is in his mid-20s. I see him sometimes at the local juice bar. He is wearing the same gray hoodie today that he wore the last time I saw him, and the time before that. I wonder what he is doing at the juice bar in the middle of the day. There is a ghostly quality to him. He is present but absent. Is he high? I can usually tell the exact drugs a person is consuming just by observing their eyes and their body posture, a skill that came in handy when I ran a young adult substance abuse program. Judging by the dullness in his eyes and by the deep body slouch, he hasn't yet smoked the weed he loves so much this morning.

A woman arrives, who seems to be an old high school friend. There is lightness in her eyes and a vibrancy in the way she engages with him and the people around her. She clearly has made something of her life. He clearly has not.

After she leaves, I see him playing a video game on his phone. His eyes light up briefly, but not for long. They have a weak glimmer, like a bad shoeshine done quickly and with no real effort.

He pushes his matted hair away from his face. My guess is he hasn't showered in a couple of days. I don't even have to guess whether he has a job or not. No way. He has no job, he has no power. His sweatshirt stinks, his hair stinks, his body stinks, his life stinks.

Still, he's drinking a smoothie. He's trying to be healthy. Maybe he'll make something out of today after all. Maybe he will finish that application and send it out. Most likely not. He will get high before midday, whether he wants to or not. His promises, his affirmations, his goals will go up in smoke along with his blunt. He will play video games for the rest of the day, perhaps for the rest of the decade. To look at our guy is to take in what true lack of purpose and power really is.

Away he goes, like a leaf in the wind, back to his parents' house or some apartment they are paying for. The people who love him watch as he blows, keeping hope that one day he will find a reason for his life and the power to fight.

Our guy is not alone. As an addiction counselor, I am a daily witness to the struggle that so many young men experience as they seek independence and true happiness. Too many of them are getting trapped in the stage between boyhood and adulthood.

The thirty-year-old who has been having a few drinks every day, now drinks around the clock and has lost nearly everything. He still lives with his parents. The twenty-year-old who just failed out of his second college has no job, no sense of purpose, no independence and no happiness. He also has no idea what happened to him. He was once a happy kid! Now he doesn't even want to get out of bed in the morning and has no reason to do so. For him, this has happened in the blink of an eye.

This state of apathy is especially true for "emerging men" — males between age 16 and 35. This stage of life is a threshold, a natural and also challenging passage from boyhood to manhood. If you look at the results today, we are miserably failing these threshold men. It has quickly gone from being a stage of emergence to a *state of emergency*. We are a nation watching as our young men flail and ultimately sink.

Looking at this, you can't help but ask: How are young men like this getting lured and trapped into states of weakness, confusion and powerlessness? And, what will help them out of their prison?

Will a rational approach help, like sitting them down and talking about their goals in life? What about giving them the skills to move on? Or giving them therapy to help them understand the emotions they are having? It all sounds pretty reasonable, and this is mostly what is being offered to emerging men who are stuck.

When he was young, our guy played a board game while a doctor observed him. Later, he sat on a couch or chair and talked about his issues and how he felt about things. Since then, he has been sent, sometimes willingly and sometimes not, to various programs. He has been encouraged or even forced to take medications. And yet, look at where he is. He is slightly better off, but these methods did not lead to the mighty change.

If you ask any of these young men if what they are doing is right, or if they are happy with their life, they will say 'no.' So what's the problem? Why doesn't he move on and move out?

The reason the boy doesn't grow up and the slacker doesn't move out is the same: they have the *rational understanding* of the need to move out, but not the *primal motivation* to do so.

For this reason, any form of help that only "treats" this situation on the rational level (i.e. skill building, talking about feelings, etc.) and not the primal level, will ultimately fall short, especially with emerging men.

Primal motivation is a type of awareness: a blend of vision, hunger, and power. Without primal motivation, our guy is trapped in states of weakness and confusion. With it, our guy can change the course of his life.

I know, because I was that guy in the hoodie at the juice bar. This book is the story of my personal journey, and the professional journey I took as an addiction recovery counselor to forge a different path with the young men I worked with, a path that activated our primal power and awakened the lion within.

PART ONE

THE PRIMAL TOOLS

Chapter 1

Leaving the Cave

Brad was barreling top speed toward his end at the clinic where I'd been working. He was taking risk after risk, had damaged his mind and his awareness with his drug use, and nothing I or anyone said even remotely reached him.

Screw it, I thought. If you can't change it, then at least let's honor it. I decided to hold a mock funeral for him.

I was young, brash, and eager, even desperate to shake up these young men who so reminded me of prior versions of myself. Brad was not allowed to say anything during the funeral because, of course, he was dead.

His groupmates were ruthlessly honest. They told the story of an arrogant and immature boy who took extreme risks in life but refused to take his chance to live.

I had invited his parents and siblings to be part of the funeral. They brought flowers, old pictures of him, mementos of their life with him and placed them next to the coffin, which was a chair with a family blanket on it.

They delivered a very touching eulogy. At one point I told Brad to look at what his family had brought. He sat there, indifferently looking at matchbox cars from his childhood.

The family also brought in pictures of Brad as a young child. One of the photos was him sitting on the sand at the beach, beaming with a smile from ear to ear. How poignant it was to see what started as a happy kid filled with joy and wonder, ending up like this.

"Look at your smile in this picture," I said. "Do you remember what you were feeling?"

He just slouched in his chair-coffin, his face blank.

So, I told him to look at his family. He resisted, but I refused to give in. Finally, he turned and looked at his parents. I saw him go through the layers of denial, the armor that was keeping him from his heart. His thick veneer was starting to crack. At one point, he closed his eyes. I saw his lips shaking.

"I want to say something to them," he said, almost at a whisper.

"What's that?" I asked.

Desperately struggling to hold his tears back, he could barely speak. "I want to say . . . I'm sorry."

You could feel how badly he wanted to make contact with his family, how much he loved them and wanted their love, and he'd finally realized it. He wanted to fix his life, to be forgiven and loved.

The family and group members gazed at each other in total silence, witnessing this glimmer of hope. I wanted to congratulate them on a group well done, but I sensed that it was premature. Like most young men, Brad wanted to be pardoned, not perfected. A true transformation would require hard work and change.

"No. You cannot," I said sternly. "You're dead. And all that you and your family are left with is your wishes and memories."

Well, news travels fast in hospitals and rehabs. When the group was over, a picket line of angry nurses and social workers gathered outside my office, demanding I be reprimanded or even fired. They said my tactics were outdated and barbaric.

Even though I was scared of being fired, I sensed my approach was right. Something needed to be done, even if I didn't quite know what I was doing.

Afterward, the group members and the family — including the deceased — sincerely thanked me for my directness and for refusing to play with kid gloves.

My guerrilla tactics didn't stop. The clients at the clinic

joked that my group was called "Death Row" because of how strongly I challenged people to change. I was interested in movement, not maintenance, and I truly believed in people's ability to change. It was well known among clients that if you did not want to hear the truth, and if you didn't want to change, stay away from Gregory. And I did manage to bring about dramatic and sweeping change.

One young guy, who fought me every step of the way but who eventually found his recovery, told me, "You are either a mad man . . . or a genius. Either way, what you do works."

I guess it was his way of thanking me.

When I eventually left to start my own practice, the young men who gravitated toward my raw, direct style naturally followed me. During the first years of private practice, I had some small successes, but not like in rehab. I was left feeling frustrated and dissatisfied. All that work and time, all those sessions, just to get a client to take his meds? Make his bed?

I knew that partially the problem was lack of sticking power. When these men left the controlled, structured and supportive rehab settings, they usually fell off. But there had to be a way forward, something that would truly produce the mighty change.

I was doing some contract work in a sober living facility and got a call one morning from the sober living, asking if I could attend a meeting between one of our clients, his family, and a prominent Manhattan psychiatrist.

They were talking about Keith. I had met this client the previous week, and we'd made a brief but meaningful connection. I had engaged and challenged him one day, and he seemed to really take it in.

When I met with the psychiatrist beforehand, he laid out his plan for the client to be sent to a long-term supportive environment for the mentally ill.

I was stunned. Keith had not seemed that far gone to me. I was still processing the psychiatrist's ideas when the family arrived.

During the meeting, Keith was visibly uncomfortable. At one point, his mother put her hand on his back, and he recoiled and almost jumped off the couch. I saw that he was petrified, scared, and ashamed. It was easy to understand why. It is humbling to be a grown man in a room with your parents and doctor discussing your life. The psychiatrist shared his vision for Keith.

"You know, we could continue to keep doing this, going around in circles, but ultimately he just cannot function independently. He is going to need to go away somewhere."

He pulled out a brochure and started describing the amenities of "somewhere," including the indefinite length of stay.

As I sat and listened, I couldn't get the first meeting with this client out of my head. He had given off a different energy. I felt he could do better. I felt he could try harder. Finally, I turned to Keith and pointed to the brochure.

"You know, if you're not careful, you are going to end up at this place."

"Don't say that!" snapped the psychiatrist. "Don't frame this as something negative that he needs to be ashamed of!"

Even though I disagreed and wanted to argue, I knew my role in this meeting, so I held my tongue. The first call I made after the meeting was to the owners of the sober house.

"Guys, I really don't agree with this. I think I can crack the code with Keith. Will you let me work with him more regularly?"

They agreed, so my next call was to the parents. They were very sweet people and loved their son deeply. They had watched him suffer for years and had felt all the anguish along with him. They had already tried many different forms of treatment: inpatient hospitalization, substance abuse rehabs, sober livings, therapy, medication and more. But like me, they still believed in their son. I asked for their support to meet with Keith more regularly. The only thing I did know for sure is that I was going to have to spend more time with him. They agreed to my idea.

The first meetings were terrible. We sat in a tiny office with no windows. I tried to engage him in traditional talk and used all the methods and interventions I knew of, but he was very withdrawn, non-verbal, and low energy. Finally, out of a mix of boredom, frustration and hope, I said to Keith, "We need to leave the office. Let's go outside and do something."

That simple decision — to leave the office — became the domino that set off a chain reaction.

Chapter 2

The Walking Cure

It was awkward between us in the beginning. I didn't know what this guy liked to do. I know what I like to do in my spare time. Go for a run. Walk in the woods. Grab a cup of coffee.

One day, I asked if Keith wanted to go for a coffee. He agreed, but it turned out he didn't really like coffee and he didn't order anything. We just sat there, trying to make small talk.

He hadn't showered in a long time. His hair was matted, and he hadn't had a haircut in many months. He was close to 30 and could've been a good-looking guy, but he looked ghostly. If I would've told him to stomp a twig in half, he wouldn't have had the force to do it; that's how weak he seemed. I could almost see why his psychiatrist wanted to put him away forever.

The next meetings weren't much better, if he showed up at all. He was frozen. I wanted to take a pick and smash away the ice around him, to dig into his core, but I sensed my usual Rambo methods would've gone nowhere.

Somewhere in the midst of this, we identified some things he liked to do. He enjoyed yoga classes, and he actually did like going out to eat too. He wasn't willing to venture far, though, not beyond his block. Fortunately, there was a yoga class on his block and a restaurant he liked at the corner.

We made a rhythm of going for yoga and then going out to eat. It made it much easier to talk. We could discuss the yoga teacher, or which body parts felt sore, the various poses. Somehow, it came up that he was a big hockey fan, so we talked about hockey a lot, especially his favorite team. In my down time, I started to expose myself more to hockey on TV and in the news so that I would be able to engage more in the conversations.

We fell into this weekly routine: a yoga class and eating afterward. Sometimes we'd take a walk around the block and sit by the river and shoot the breeze. It was relaxed. We were hanging out. There was no agenda of topics that had to be covered. It didn't matter what we talked about, as long as it was enjoyable, spontaneous and real. Both of us revealed ourselves. There was an energy moving between us, and an energy moving out in the world. That movement and exchange of energy felt very promising, and important.

That's how we spent our Wednesdays for the next two years. It was the most progress he could take. Meanwhile, I referred him to a new psychiatrist and helped him see a music therapist because I thought it might open him up a bit more.

We celebrated any victories as they came, no matter how small they appeared on the surface. It was huge when he started coming on time. It was huge when he showed up at all. It was huge when he cared enough to give me the heads up to say he couldn't make it that day. He was starting to develop empathy and a sense of personal responsibility.

Probably around year three, Keith started showering regularly and getting his hair groomed. Together, we began to venture off his block. He liked art, so we went to various galleries. And we'd check out many different ethnic restaurants in the neighborhood — Mexican, Venezuelan, Italian. He started getting comfortable with the terrain, as in, "I know this restaurant here. I'm really in the mood to check out this gallery." He was creating a mental map of the world.

One day, I asked him to invite someone from the sober facility to join us for lunch. In this way, we had a shared experience in the social world, something I would normally never get to see with a client.

You know when you're trying to start a fire in the wilderness, and all you see are little sparks? I glimpsed them, like when he chose the activity we were going to do, or when he knew I wasn't feeling well and asked, genuinely, how are you feeling?

Keith knew a lot about me: the names of my children, that my father moved to America from Greece, and that I'd got into an argument with my wife the previous night. I let Keith live a little in my own life before he could live in his own. It activated his own hunger to create his own life. I liken it to a pregnancy, where the baby lives in you before they can live in the world by themselves.

The healthier he got, the more connected we became, the more he was willing to roam. Eventually, he made it to different parts of Manhattan, not just the section he lived in. When I tried to help get him a job, he'd balk. Finally, after three years, he took a small job — not a dream job, just a job, something to do.

The more he created a world for himself, the easier it was to see when he was getting stuck on a theme. Once, we went for a walk. We found a small, well-shaded park right by the river. I was really digging into him about his sense of shame which I had seen coming up. By now I had earned his trust and would often challenge him.

I said, "It's obvious to me that you're stuck, because you don't think you're worth having a good life."

He started to cry in the park, and he was someone who never expressed any emotion. I was scaring him and supporting him at the same time.

He started applying to more jobs and got a position making good money, with health insurance and vacation time. A real job. He developed a serious relationship with a woman. He made some friends and cultivated new hobbies. Now he's sober. But he needs to level up again, I tell him, or life will pass him by.

I learned a lot from working with Keith. I learned — not the talking cure, as Freud phrased it, but the walking cure — the power of leaving the office and getting to know and see young men in action (or inaction) in the social world.

I love to do things, be on the move. Maybe that's why simply talking was never enough or just frustrating, and why the transition from the office to the outdoors was so powerful for me.

I experienced and still experience the office as stagnant and fixed, never changing. It is also very one-sided, in the sense that it "belongs" to someone, and the other person is a "visitor." This immediately and perhaps intentionally sets up a hierarchy, where one person is smarter, stronger and wiser than the other, and not by virtue of fact or reality, but simply by ownership and title. Office space is separate from the world — a clinical, controlled environment. In its essence, it's limited.

Outside, on the other hand, is vibrant and exciting, unpredictable. You never know what to expect. A rabbit crossing your path, a policeman ticketing you for jaywalking, a child trying to walk to his mother. At its essence is abundance. You are facing the wild, organic world alongside one another, equally instead of hierarchically. No one person is investigating the other. The psyche can relax a little; it isn't as guarded. The whole environment allows for more change, fluidity, malleability. Once I experienced the power of working with young men outside, I never wanted to go back.

Chapter 3

The Mirror Effect

Being outside, just hanging out, connecting while doing things together created this relaxed vibe. Without the goal-oriented pressure of therapy — like talking about and processing difficult emotions, discussing your barriers to achieving your dreams in life, reviewing your past — it was almost like both of our psyches just chilled out. With a relaxed psyche and mind, something amazing started to happen. We were doing things together, living life — and they were watching me. I found that being around these young men in this way subtly allowed them to see me and then repeat what they saw. I started calling this "the mirror effect."

* * *

When I was about 15, a young couple moved from the Boston area into my neighborhood. The man, Chris, was Irish American. He had dark auburn hair, a nice tan, and was in his mid-thirties. He worked in Manhattan and made good money. He was into all sports and was a huge fan of Boston teams. He drove a Kelly-green Porsche and he smoked cigarettes — not a wimpy cigarette like a Parliament Lights, but the no-filter Camels. He just had this vibe I wanted to be around. He was such a cool guy.

I went to his house constantly to play basketball with him, watch sports together, and just talk. He had what would now be called a man cave. A big TV. Sports posters and memorabilia. A wet bar.

When I went into that back room, the energy shifted. This wasn't a place where families would be watching *Frozen* or *Moana*. It was the Boston Bruins, the Boston Celtics, the Boston Red Sox. Or the Patriots. It had the feeling of maleness and warmth.

I loved hanging out with him, so much so that I would go there whenever I felt like it. Sometimes, while standing at the door, I would hear him groaning to his wife, "I want to watch the game. I just don't want to be around him right now."

But his sweetheart wife was on my side. I would stand patiently by the door like an eager puppy while she would soothe through his resistance.

"Chris, he's just a kid. He sees you as a role model."

She would plead until he finally would allow me into their house.

He had such an unabashed pursuit of his goals, whatever they happened to be. For instance, he had a goal to dunk on the hoop nailed into the side of his garage. The hoop was ten feet high, and he was your basic white guy, five foot nine. He just didn't have the vertical leap. Funny enough, having grown up in the Air Jordan era of basketball, I also had that same goal. I also wanted to fly and dreamed of being able to dunk.

One day, Chris had us both take the bench from his picnic table and put it in his driveway, right under the hoop. His plan was to run toward the hoop, place one foot on the bench which would give him another twelve inches, and dunk it. So, I'm videotaping this as he runs toward the hoop, plants his foot on the bench, gets up and — yes! He dunks the ball!

All of a sudden, I hear a loud sound of wood breaking. The hoop came crashing to the ground, taking half of the garage down with it. And I caught it all on video.

That sound of the wood crashing to the ground was the funniest thing I'd ever heard. But what really stayed with me was how he went about making his dream a reality. No matter how it got done, he made it happen.

What I got from Chris was that being a man is fun. I'd

think to myself: If I were to grow up to be this guy, that would be okay. He was good-looking and had a smart, beautiful wife and two beautiful kids. He didn't seem broken by the grind of life. Men feel they've traded their freedom for this American Dream, the family life. And then they end up feeling shackled to responsibility. Too much responsibility. But Chris, he gave me something to look forward to. Chris embodied what my technique aims to do: give a young man a vision of what he can be by merely spending time with each other.

It turns out that living your life alongside another man, so that he can see, feel, hear what maleness looks like is more powerful than I realized.

After I had been using this technique for a while, I came across research about the brain that blew me away. The brain has an entire system, the mirror neuron system, that stimulates growth and change. When two people are in regular contact with each other, there is a mirroring effect, meaning they will be influenced by the other person's energy and direction.

Because our brains mirror one another, we influence one another — that is our power and our magic together. This is why mirroring and simply "hanging out" are so vital and powerful. Amazingly, when a man sees an alternative way of living, it stimulates and even impregnates the part of his mind that forms images. He cannot help but start to visualize and see — and vision leads to action, for what we see in our minds, we manifest in our life. Monkey see, monkey do. Man see, man do. We men mimic and eventually become what we see, both internally and externally.

When we consider what is going on in the brain beneath the surface, the power of presence — of simply hanging out — is truly revolutionary. The process of a man learning about himself begins when he sees his reflection by looking at another man. That's why I was so inexplicably drawn to Chris. My mind was unconsciously taking notes, assimilating facts: this is how a man looks and sounds, this is how a man laughs with his whole body, this is how a man humbles himself before his wife when he has really screwed up, this is how a man goes to bat for his learning-disabled child, this is how a man prays or shaves or a million other things.

This is why living alongside another man is crucial for male development. Seeing another man in motion, engaged in a task or interacting with the social world — all this activates your own image of yourself and who you might be.

But, we are not just talking about any man. This man must be in touch with his authentic self. This man must have heart and passion, and be taking his heart full on into life. Looking at him, you feel that this man is enjoying life. There is a freedom and joy about him. This man must be a *mentor*.

What is a mentor? I define a mentor as simply someone who is further along the path than you are — usually someone older than you who has walked the path before you.

This man can be found in sports, work, hobbies, neighborhoods, families. And if possible, threshold men should find more than one. Don't worry if the mentor is nice or coddles you. Even if he's hard on you, does he care about you? Does he want to pour into you some of what he is made of? If he does, that is generally the right mentor.

I discovered that the process of mentoring can be made as deep and complex as we wish, but at its simplest and most fundamental level, the most important thing any mentor can do for an emerging man is just to be present, and then trust his power and the process.

Like Chris, I needed to be a living, moving presence in young men's lives, and at the same time to find a subtle way to showcase myself and my power.

Or so I thought. There was still a big gap in my approach.

Chapter 4

Miyagi Mentoring

Through the mirror effect, the young men I worked with were changing slowly. But I could still see a huge barrier to their success in life. It was like they were in the classroom of life, not understanding. Then they'd eventually give up and always get sent to the principal's office. But why were they so stuck? They were frustrated, and I was frustrated. It was time to pay a visit to an old friend.

I was a young boy when the movie *The Karate Kid* came out. The story centers around Daniel and his single mom who move to a new town. Almost immediately, Daniel becomes a target by a gang of local boys who practice karate. He is getting beaten to a pulp one day when Mr. Miyagi, the elderly handyman at his apartment complex, expertly fights off the gang and rescues Daniel.

Daniel eventually becomes aware that Mr. Miyagi is a master of karate himself and pleads with the man to teach him martial arts. Finally, Mr. Miyagi consents, demanding Daniel's total commitment. No questions, just do.

For the next few days, he instructs Daniel to wax his car (wax on, wax off), paint his fence (up, down), sand the floor (side to side), and other menial and sometimes humiliating tasks that have nothing to do with karate.

Daniel resentfully complies, until finally he can't take it anymore. In a dramatic moment of the story, Daniel threatens to quit, at which point Mr. Miyagi shows Daniel how each task secretly correlated to essential moves in karate. Painting the fence is how to block a punch; waxing is how to block a kick.

Like boys all over the world, I was crazy about the movie. I was struck by how Mr. Miyagi approached his apprentice — casual, secretly. He was teaching without teaching, or as Bruce Lee called it, "the art of fighting without fighting." Miyagi geared his lessons to Daniel's individual person. And it all happened not at school or at a gym but in Mr. Miyagi's backyard, this deep connecting between the master and the student. It was almost like a transfer of energy.

I was entranced by how Mr. Miyagi incorporated lessons based around what life required; he needed his fence painted, so he taught blocking through painting; needed his cars buffed, so ditto. He used the ocean to teach balance and humility. If it's there, it can be used. And if at first Mr. Miyagi's requests seemed self-serving, Daniel soon realized that whatever he asked was for Daniel's ultimate benefit.

What was the karate master doing? Opposing Daniel. Giving him a model of strength and restraint. A model of total commitment. What it means to humble yourself to the task and give it your all, even if it doesn't seem to make sense to you. He was teaching not only karate, but life.

When I started my work with young men, I kept thinking of Mr. Miyagi. Most of the therapy approaches I knew tackled obstacles directly. Miyagi made me realize that in the hands of a master, all acts — baking bread, watching sports, washing the car — become imbued with healing power. And I dared myself to incorporate that concept in my own work. I called it Miyagi Mentoring.

The trick was finding the ordinary act that would reach that particular individual. With Devon, a practitioner of jiu-jitsu, it was easy. We wrestled. Scott loved basketball, so we joined the gym and played. But it was not always that straightforward. For Andy, the solution came while we were hiking in the mountains.

Andy was a massive man with the impulse control of a rabid animal. As we were hiking, we happened to cross paths with a group of deer. They were eating awfully close to us, and we both had the same idea: Let's see how close we can get.

We both crouched down, slowly planting each foot, step by step, carefully and stealthily moving like predators in the wild. I was amazed! I just stopped and watched this "out-of-control" addict calmly slither through the woods and damn near touch those animals. I couldn't have come up with a better way teach a man to learn control of his mind and body!

Sometimes in Miyagi Mentoring, we make ourselves the student in front of the clients, to show them how it's done. These Miyagi acts have stakes on both ends. I ask men to take risks, but I also model my own willingness to take risks and make sacrifices — that is part of the mirror effect.

One of my clients was struggling to stay sober. I sensed he was on the cusp, that if he decided to stay sober he could do it. I worked it from all angles, trying to convince him to try sobriety. We had built up enough mutual trust so that I could say, "I'll tell you what, Jack. You think you can stay sober? Do it. Give me this summer sober. If you fail, you agree that we ramp up your recovery. Either you go to rehab or balls to the wall in AA."

"Okay," he said. "But what happens if I succeed?"

"What do you mean?" I said.

"Well, if I fall short, I have consequences. What about you? If I succeed, what happens to you?"

"Well, you get to experience the gift. It is for you, not for me."

He gave me a "c'mon, bro" look. Okay, what he wanted was some skin in the game from me.

"Fine," I said. "If you succeed, you choose two things that I might do." I was thinking along the lines of taking him out for a very expensive sushi dinner. Jack had other ideas.

"I only have one thing: skydiving."

My heart sank when he said it. I hate surrendering my life into something other than myself, and he knew it. I tried to change his mind, but he insisted, so we were on.

Well, Jack did stay sober that summer. I remember thinking as I landed on the ground after jumping out of the plane: I am asking these guys to take huge risks and essentially jump out of a plane and trust me that a new life awaits them. Give up drugs, the lifestyle, and a new life awaits. I know that the new life is there, but they don't. I need to be willing to jump out of the plane as well.

What I discovered through my in-motion method was, I don't need to be a sensei or Mr. Miyagi to have a huge impact. I need to find a way to connect young men to tasks that can teach them. I discovered this is yet another method of many to guide my guy to his own power. Whether it be jiu-jitsu, skateboarding, basketball, meditation or plumbing, all methods have the power to teach.

And I don't always need to be doing the teaching. Part of my evolution was realizing when to be the Miyagi, and when to find one.

Chapter 5

Finding a Miyagi

I met Larry when he was 19. Larry was tall and lanky and had an analytical mind that helped him in school but kept him from real feelings and life experiences. He was always second guessing himself — and life — to an extreme.

Because he felt he couldn't control life, that's exactly what he tried to do. He had a bad case of Goldilocks Syndrome. Whatever we did, it wasn't quite right. If we went hiking, it was too cold, or too hot, or too windy. If we went to a restaurant, the wait was too long. No to basketball because of a blister on his foot.

All of this led to Larry being stuck in himself. You could see that he was ingrown, lost in his own thoughts about the world and about people, and even about himself. He had no real experience of anything, only paralyzing reservations about those potential experiences.

The greatest antidote to the stuck, separate self is to get into action in the social world. I wracked my brain to come up with activities that he'd enjoy. I suggested running, painting, cooking, jiu-jitsu. Finally, nearly out of ideas, I suggested surfing.

I saw a mix of excitement and fear, a glimmer of interest, but then he shook his head no. When I probed, he admitted that a couple of years ago he'd gone surfing, or tried to, but after two minutes in the ocean, the surfboard had whacked him on the chin. The following summer, he tried lessons with a pro, but the surfer had Larry practice all these techniques at the beach: how to pop the board, when to jump on, how to keep your feet on, etc. He couldn't get it at all. He said he had his fill of surfing.

Over the weeks, I tried to pique his interest. Larry would come back with all these reasons he would make a lousy surfer, but I noticed he didn't dismiss it outright.

Using my Miyagi Mentoring, I knew my best shot was getting the right teacher. If I couldn't be that for Larry, then I needed to find the one person who could.

After asking around, I heard from a friend about a local guy. The description was perfect, so I gave him a call. We talked for a bit, and he told me about all the surfing adventures he'd gone on. He'd told me he was married, so I found myself wondering, "How the hell do you get 'permission' to go all over the world surfing?" I finally asked Marc.

"Simple. I have a surfing pre-nuptial."

I had to hear this one.

"Before I got married," he explained, "I told my wife, 'I will never cheat on you. I will always provide for you. But I am a surfer. I need these two weeks each year to go surfing.'"

I knew instantly this was our guy.

We all met at the beach. It was a beautiful sunny day but with enough wind to have some really nice waves. The whole way to the beach I had to listen to Larry moan about how it wasn't going to work; he had tried everything — and of course by "everything" he meant the board smacked him in the head once, and he had one bad lesson.

The surfing instructor showed up. He was about sixty years old without an ounce of flab on him. He was totally relaxed and smiling.

Marc took a moment, looked Larry up and down, and said, "Bro, I won't teach you anything. I don't want you to think about anything."

Larry looked surprised but then nodded.

Marc put his hand on Larry's shoulder and said, "Just hook the board onto your leg and go out. Go feel the water." Then he sent Larry off.

After the first few waves, Marc swam over to Larry. This was the only piece of instruction I heard him give. "It's all about balance. If you're too close to the front of the surfboard, you'll nosedive. If you're too far back, the nose will fly up. You need to be in the exact spot you need to be. Now go out and feel the balance."

Larry went back and took the next wave. Not bad.

The instructor swam over. "Bro, you're doing only one thing wrong. Do you feel what it is?"

Larry squinted, then nodded. It wasn't a fake nod. He really did seem to feel what it was, because when he caught the next wave, Larry surfed! And kept surfing.

It was amazing to see him in perfect balance. It was like his brain was turned off and the rest of him was turned on. I watched him paddle out, looking for the right wave, then when he found it, he'd start paddling furiously until just the moment when it crested and he found a way to snap to his feet. He was getting his feel for the board, his body, the water. It was a symphony around him. Larry was the maestro leading it all and being led, not controlling anything.

When Larry came to shore, he just sat there silent and smiling. I knew something was working deep within him.

When it was time to leave, Larry brushed the sand off the board and put it under his arm. No complaining. We sat on the sand, watching the waves roll in while silhouettes of surfers were bobbing up and down, sometimes taking waves.

Larry was watching all this, then he turned to Marc, who was nearby packing up some of his gear, and asked, "So, why do people love surfing so much?"

"You know, the way I look at it," Marc said, jutting his chin to the sky, "the sun is 98 million miles away, and it is sending these rays to the earth, which creates the atmosphere and interacts with the moon, the water, everything. And it creates a ripple, which becomes a wave. And that wave slowly starts rolling to the shore. That wave is the final moment of a 98-million-mile journey. And we get to ride that. That's what surfing is. And I love that!"

Then he launched into some tales about surfing, places he'd been. He told a story about surfing at night in Nicaragua, under the full moon, seeing shooting stars.

Larry just sat there listening to Marc, his love for surfing, and the way he saw the world. If Marc had shared any of this beforehand, it would have totally missed Larry. But now he got it.

The instructor had said he wasn't going to teach Larry anything, but through him Larry learned that surfing is about feeling your way through, instinctually. It's about moving through the waves, the mess, the craziness, the danger and fear, and not losing your footing.

Over the years, I've noticed many of the surfers I've met are extremely spiritual. They have to be, to get to that point of being one with the elements. To move in the eye of the storm, you have to have that sense of spiritual union with the universe. It's even more crucial than balance.

Marc seemed to recognize something about Larry, and Larry recognized something about him. He was providing some crucial male stuff by osmosis. He was helping Larry make the leap from merely having a transaction with the world to having a real connection.

And yet, all these one-on-one connections could do only so much, could only go so far. To take the next step, we had to connect to a community.

Chapter 6

Enter the Agora

With some exceptions, most forms of therapy operate on what I call the Dialogic Axis, or the talking axis. It relies on the power of two people talking, especially in a logical and critical way. "Why do you think you did that?" "What did that incident bring up for you?" "How can you arrange to get up on time in the morning?" These are all great questions, mostly aimed at the rational mind.

But the cognitive part of young males' brains is not fully developed at that age. The young men I encountered didn't have the capacity to reflect and process verbally, or had little interest in learning how. This led me to come up with an alternative approach that I dubbed the Diakinetic Axis, or the action axis. Diakinetic means *with motion* or *with movement*. This Diakinetic Axis, in contrast to the Dialogic Axis, uses action instead of reason, talking, or logic as its mode of transmission.

So, you don't want to talk, or you can't talk? Fine. Let's walk and see what happens. No agenda. Let's hang out together. Most often the "talking" comes if it needs to, but in the natural rhythm of life and living.

The more I walked with clients, I saw that it was not just about moving. There was some power that we were tapping into in the social world.

As a Greek, I know the healing power of the social gathering place, called the agora. The agora is the meeting place, a trading ground where everything is shared from food, to ideas, to art and music. We gather there and rejoice — and we fight there too. No matter, though, because we keep coming back to the agora.

In essence, by two people facing the world alongside one another instead of only facing each other, they share an experience in the social world and create a special bond. I am amazed by the healing that happens when I use this "alongside" technique with an emerging man, getting him into action and exploring the social world together with me.

This phase of development, what I call primal exploring, is about getting physically active in the world and also being open — really open — to new experiences, so that they can start to penetrate the person. By that,

I mean you aren't just going through the motions of life, but actually allowing life to go through you, so you can experience what's before you to the fullest. It's the difference between reading a book about climbing Mt. Kilimanjaro and actually doing it. Climbing the mountain requires you to feel the sharp wind on your face, to have a morning tea before the magical sunrise, to witness the smiles on the sherpas' faces as they pack, and the elation when you finally see the summit.

I learned that both diakinetic and dialogic work are necessary, and they can be complementary, especially if diakinetic work comes before the rational work. You can take a guy mountain climbing, or hiking, or to a yoga class, or cook with him and then ask him questions about what he did.

The aim of the exploration stage is to get the person involved in life and in the social world. That is a big step for most emerging men who have become conditioned to hide in their "safe" comfortable space — their zoo.

* * *

When I started working together with Jose, he told me that he enjoyed kickboxing.

"That's great," I said. "Where do you work out?"

"At my home. My trainer comes there, and we work out in my living room."

"Oh, so about how many rounds do you do?"

"Around nine or so," he replied.

I looked at him, skeptical. He was fairly fit, but to pull off nine rounds — I don't know. I had my doubts. Even if his self-assessment was correct, I thought he would be better off in an actual gym.

The gyms of my own youth are still alive inside me. The genders were divided then. The women got the room with the nautilus equipment, the ellipticals and bikes and the machines. The men occupied the room with the free weights.

In the free-weight room, there was no air conditioning. It was very small, and hot. It felt like a male womb. These were tough men, huge men, double the size of me. I absolutely loved it.

The music there was turned up really loud — heavy metal or classic rock. Nobody else entered unless they had to. Even the head of the gym would tiptoe in feebly to voice other members' complaints about the loud music.

Back then, the guys working out weren't doing it to impress anybody. Except for the cursing, you didn't really say anything. You had to silently negotiate how long you'd be on the equipment. You had to negotiate everything non-verbally. These men did not want to talk to you; they didn't want you getting in their way, interrupting them. They were on personal business.

There was a very clear hierarchy, a pecking order. Everyone knew who the alpha men were. The guys that were older, in their forties and fifties, their energy set the tone. You wouldn't have a 21-year-old come in and disrupt that. The hierarchy was based on how strong you were as a male. Of course, you could have a skinny guy who was very male too, as long as he had that male essence to him.

Some guys at the gym were clearly all about looks. They were often on steroids, and those juice heads were not respected. You could tell they were trying to cover over their lack of masculinity with muscles. You could feel their insecurity, that they were trying to prove something, not to themselves, but to others.

Most gyms of today are nothing like the gyms of my youth, so you have to search for the right gym — and by "right" I mean something that can breathe life into you. The problem too many guys face is that they choose a gym in the same way they choose everything in life: to keep their ego exactly as it is. Well, if you choose life that way, it has no ability to penetrate you.

After a short search, I found the perfect place for Jose

and me. The first day we met with our trainer was fantastic! He worked us out hard. I looked over, and Jose was sitting on the floor, drenched with sweat, panting, face beet red. He was done. We had barely done one full round.

I smiled. What happened to Jose's nine rounds?

We learned so many things that day. Of course, we had fun and had a great workout. We also connected to a new place of power. But at a deeper level, we engaged with and faced reality. Jose learned what "a round" really is, and that he could only do one round, not nine.

The trainer was very caring and motivational, but he was firm and realistic. A round is you hitting the pads or the bag for three minutes. A round doesn't end after thirty seconds because you're tired. It ends when it ends.

If you live in reality, you can start to measure your progress because the road is set. It doesn't change based on how you feel or what you want that day.

Today, the agora's healing power is greatly under-used. For the most part, modern culture is not celebrating the agora, although there are exceptions. In Greece, for example, they shut down a major six-lane road that circles the Acropolis and made it into a cobbled pedestrian road where people can walk, play music, eat outdoors.

Other cultures have also understood the importance of the agora. I once heard that in one African tribe they mark the child's birth as the moment a woman first thinks of having a child. On that moment, she goes out to a tree and the tree teaches her the song of her future child. She then teaches that song to the father. They both sing the song to the child as he or she comes into the world. And, demonstrating the power of the agora, the entire village is taught the song. If at any time in that child's life they start to go astray and lead an immoral life, the child sits in the center of a circle created by the village, and they all sing the song — their song — back to them.

Today, we aren't born into agoras. We are a society of individuals. We have to look for and build the agora. In America, we think we are in agoras when we join Facebook groups, but agoras need to be physical. We need to be in each others' presence, pick up on the vibes. Join the running group. Volunteer at the animal shelter. My wife goes to a pottery group every Thursday where people across three generations make their own cups and plates and have lunch together. Get involved in society. Find the community that breathes fresh life into you. In this way, you will build a life.

We found the power of community, of the agora. But is that enough? I kept questioning myself, pushing myself and my clients to the limit, trying to figure out what would truly bring about the mighty change.

Chapter 7

Emphatic Challenge

When I was a junior in high school, I made the decision to switch from soccer to American football. I had played tackle football in the snow for years and I was really good. So how hard could football be?

Well, transitioning to football turned out to be very difficult and trying. The pads felt heavy and cumbersome. I felt slow and weak. I was completely out of my element.

I remember one of the first padded practices where we hit each other. Toward the end of practice, we ran a drill called "the gauntlet," where a runner has the ball and charges through rows of resisters who lower themselves and hit the runner. The goal is to advance through four rows of two people.

I took the ball and started casually running towards the lines of men. The first duo included the team captain, a country boy: big, thick, strong, and tough. As I trotted aimlessly towards him, he lowered himself and sent me back about three yards. "Get lower!" he screamed. Shocked, I re-collected myself and ran back at the line. He knocked me back again and said, "Get lower!" I ran towards the line again, and he lowered and knocked me back yet again: "Get lower!"

Finally, channeling all my power and all my might, I lowered myself, bit into my mouthpiece and charged screaming towards the line. I drove through him and the rest of the lines.

He gave me a vital lesson that day. As a newcomer to the sport, I needed the team captain's firm introduction to power, particularly male power. Each blow he gave me not only taught me how to run in football, it taught me how to be a football player. Each blow had a force, a statement to it.

Blow one: You are a soccer player. Go back to soccer!

Blow two: You don't really want to be here. You just think you want to be here.

Blow three: This is a tryout. Nothing is guaranteed. Show me, convince me, that you are fit for this game.

It was as if the team captain was sending me a message I would only understand and appreciate at some point in the future: "You have to come through me. Your strength must be activated — for your good as well as my own."

Until he trained and challenged me as a growing man,

I did not realize I had that much power inside me. I did not know that I needed it, or how to get it.

This process of men emphatically challenging boys has mostly disappeared today. In its place is empathic support. I get it. That kind of support might have been absent in the past, and probably caused terrible damage. But today, the softer approach is reflexively offered and grossly overused. In fact, both are necessary — *empathic support* and *emphatic challenge*.

That tough boy who blocked me in high school? Today, he would be sat down and told, "Hey, c'mon, man. This guy just started. Give him break." And if the team captain had done just that, he would've interrupted my own power story. He would've robbed me of a thrilling and transformative life lesson.

I'll never forget that lesson, because it is mind-blowing to discover your own strength, courage, and ingenuity. It is the discovery of how much more you can be and do — more than you could have possibly imagined! Emphatic challenge is necessary to male growth, and does not always need to come in one massive blow.

I was traveling by train in Japan one day when I saw massive clusters of bushes through the windows. They were three to five feet tall and looked to be the most vibrant green imaginable. Later, I learned that they were actually trees — tea trees. Left untouched, they can grow to between thirty and sixty feet high. The way the tea farmers get the tree to have such a concentration of color and flavor is by pruning. They cut the branches back, so all that tea energy gets concentrated into the smallest space. And that process produces the finest tea.

By intelligently and lovingly pruning the male tree, the cutting back creates growth. It's the 'cutting back' and not the 'cutting down.' Without that tough country boy on the football team opposing me, I never would have contacted my deeper core, my willpower. Without emphatic challenge, there is nothing to activate the spirit.

And it's not that boys today lack adversity. There is plenty of that. The problem is that no one consciously devotes time to challenging them. That's what the best teachers and masters of prior generations offered: discipline, direction, personal responsibility. If only there were some way to blend the best of the past with the nurturing environment of today.

It's called male training, or mentorship. Through focused and directed challenge, a young boy learns to adapt, overcome, and channel his deeper impulses, both the good ones and the bad ones. Each act of self-discipline boosts his confidence and self-respect, because he is learning to master himself and his desires. He is getting the "PhD in Me."

He doesn't just feel entitled to the riches of the universe. Instead, he feels worthy of them and goes out to fight for those riches.

Avoiding male training works . . . for a little while. I discovered it wasn't so bad to be a 15-year-old rebellious kid who refused all authority, who dropped off the baseball team because I didn't like the one coach, or gave up on guitar because the teacher wanted me to practice more. Fast forward five or ten years, to when I was still living at home and had absolutely no clue and no hope for liberating myself from mommy and daddy. Not as cool. Any 25-year-old living at home with his parents can back me up on that.

My life demonstrated to me that having other men in your life is essential to activating your maleness. It is the "yeast" of the recipe — without it, you cannot rise.

I needed another man to oppose me and challenge me. As a kid, here and there I met up with such men and gleaned what I could. But it wasn't enough, not by a long shot.

Hey, guys. Has it been enough for you? When was the last time you allowed yourself to be truly challenged and surprised yourself with your own strength, courage, ingenuity?

And hey, dads. I have an honest question for you. What do you think is going on here with your son? Look at yourself. You go to work every single day, no matter how you feel. You come back home, no matter how you feel. You made this whole dream from nothing. No one handed this life to you. So why can't your son understand and apply these basic rules to life? How come your son won't learn the ways of the world from you?

Here is my prayer, my plea and wish for all the dads out there: Tell your son your journey; share what it took to get to where you are today. That includes the highs and the lows. Tell him what got you through. Tell him honestly and humbly. Tell him your deepest hope and your most sincere concern for him. Tell him once — like it's the last thing you will ever get a chance to say to him. Then tell him you love him.

*   *   *

If males are not challenging other males, there is nothing that will activate the inner male spirit. You cannot avoid this process of being challenged, trained, mentored — not if you intend to grow. You alone cannot activate your own internal spirit. To grow, you must be challenged, opposed, even overpowered.

Today, generations of men are failing to link up. It's through this linkage that male knowledge, wisdom, and experience are imparted. The evolution of life depends on ancestral knowledge being passed, received, and internalized from one generation to the next. There is an evolutionary formula that has existed for thousands of years and is the one glaring thing missing today: Men are no longer making men.

Chapter 8

Hold the Line

I knew a young man, let's call him Bobby. He was a stubborn, self-reliant buck, constantly ramming his head into the walls of life. Whatever Bobby wanted, he either took or it was gifted to him. And he wanted it all right now. He would fall a couple of times, though the consequences of his behavior were cushioned by his well-intentioned but misguided parents. They, like most parents to boys like this, were running ahead of him with axes and picks, trying to knock down the walls before he hit them, or else running behind him with shovels and buckets to clean up the messes he made.

Put yourself in Bobby's shoes. By not feeling the consequences of his choices, his beliefs, and his way of life, his attitude became, "What's wrong with how I am living? What's wrong with my lifestyle and thinking? I don't see a problem with it."

Naturally, pal. But take a peek at your parents, who put blood, sweat, and tears into cleaning up all your crap! This is why — at least in rehabs in the past — we forced a break from this cycle. Parents' shovels, axes and other clean-up tools were confiscated. And what happens when Bobby makes a few messes and no one cleans up after him? The lights naturally come on.

"Oh man, I am basically destroying myself and everything in my path. My way doesn't work!"

Yes! Now you got it, Bobby!

Bobby got it because finally there was no one there to cushion the fall.

Emerging men like Bobby need support from outside sources. These sources can take a bird's eye view of the situation, because they aren't Bobby's parents. Mentors, coaches, neighbors, and teachers can all provide this type of outside insight. Part of that help includes holding the line when the boys want to give up. For the most part, that means family members and helping professionals need to be solid.

It is a given that if your life is out of control, someone in your life must hold the line. If you are a young man reading this, you had better hope that you have people in your life who will hold the line when you get soft and weak, which you will. These people will get you to see what you don't see, get you to believe what you don't believe, and get you to accomplish what you cannot do.

I was just plain lucky. I met someone who held the line for me. And I hated him for it for years.

* * *

There was a stretch of time when I wanted to become a professional athlete. I trained seriously for it, running and lifting weights every day for hours upon hours. I worked with personal trainers of all kinds. I was pursuing my dream and I worked very hard. Eventually, I got a football scholarship. Coaches said they never saw anyone play with such passion and ferocity.

That passion took a huge toll. My body kept getting injured. Still, I kept playing, for years. In my sophomore year of college, my body got injured so badly I couldn't play football. When that happened, I stopped caring and gave up on all my classes. So, now I had a broken body and was failing out of school too. I had given up on everything.

Then a chance encounter with an old teammate woke me and lit a fire under my ass. I trained for four months and got my body where it needed to be so I could play. But then there was the matter of my academics. I needed to make a comeback there too. But instead of patience and hard work, I resorted to plain manipulation.

All I needed was for two professors to change my F to incomplete. Then I could make up the coursework and be academically eligible to play. I went to the first professor, a professor of religion. I gave him the whole poor-me story, which included every excuse in the book. Because he was a religious guy, I think he took pity on me and gave me the incomplete.

The second professor, I felt, would be even easier. It was a huge class, probably 300 people. Why would he care either way whether I got an F or incomplete? As I walked into his office, I saw he had a cast on his arm. Perfect!

"What happened to your arm?" I asked, feigning interest.

Then I started to share my own injury saga. I tried to bond with him. It was going well. Then I gave my story: I'd had a tough semester. Lost sight of my focus. Something like that. The professor looked at me across his desk, contemplating.

"I know the easy thing to do would be to give you the incomplete," he said. "But some people in life have to stand for what is right, and I'm not going to give you the incomplete."

Those words hit me on the side of the head like a

shovel. I couldn't believe it. I tried feebly to plea with him, moaning and telling him what this meant to my life. Then I got angry and tried to make eye contact, not to enlist his sympathies but to intimidate him, let him know I might hurt him physically if he didn't change his mind. But he kept his eyes down on his desk, writing something. I felt a huge anger building in me. I just needed him to look at me! But he wouldn't lift his eyes. I finally gave up. I walked out of the office, into the courtyard outside of the building.

I sat down on the pavement. My lifelong dream of being an athlete was over. Done. I had no moves left to make. I started crying. I hadn't cried like that in years — maybe ever.

A college girl came over and interrupted my crying. "Do you know where the gym is?" she asked. I listlessly pointed to the direction where the gym was. And that was it.

I'd always imagined my final athletic act being more ceremonial, being on stage or in front of a huge audience, scoring the winning touchdown, getting a roaring applause. Instead, it was me crying in a courtyard pointing some girl toward the gym.

Even though I was devastated at my dream disintegrating and enraged at the professor, I know now that what he did was incredible. Most professors would've thought: "Let this slacker get what he wants so he can live in his imaginary life until he fails out again." Instead, he did the right thing. He was saying, "You can't manipulate your way out of this one." He was a wall. I couldn't go through him. He held the line, not with cruelty, meanness or threats, but with total conviction.

So, I fell, badly, and I experienced all the pain that came with it. It turned out, after losing the dream of playing professional sports, a gap was left inside me that ultimately ended up being filled with spirituality.

It is scary for me to think what might've happened if the professor gave me the incomplete and I had gotten reinstated. Maybe by some miracle I would have continued to play football and not injured my body. I might not have gotten back into drugs and gambling. Maybe I would have learned to show myself and others the respect they deserved. That's all great. But I still would have been the same Greg, manipulating people and sidestepping personal responsibility. Like Bobby, my takeaway would've been: Hey, my manipulating and cheating works! On the surface, I might have achieved something, but beneath that I would still be hollow and empty.

So why aren't we doing this today — challenging our young men when we know that is what they need?

Chapter 9

Let Them Suffer

As you are starting to see, the process of the mighty change is not soft and easy. With emphatic challenge, we see that it not only takes a village, it often takes a villain. And, in order to change, young men need to suffer. They need to be *allowed* to suffer.

* * *

Joey was a big bear of a guy: goofy, witty and funny too. He knew how to contort his face in hilarious ways. He had a whole menu of faces, and if he'd had more confidence, could've been a stand-up comedian. At his "job" (he worked four hours a month at his mother's travel company), he'd often see couples in relationships or on dates and longed to be in a relationship himself, but it had never happened. He didn't like his job, but he didn't absolutely hate it either. It was like an arranged marriage. He never chose it or unchose it. He was studying something difficult at school — he was a smart kid — but he didn't like that either.

At 21, he came to me because he couldn't make any friends in the real world. His only friends were the few people he played video games with. Even they had never met in person. His social world was entirely electronic. He did know a couple of people in the physical world, but he couldn't break down that barrier between him and them.

When he was young, he was a really quirky, rambunctious and energetic kid who didn't know his own limits. Like so many young boys these days, he was diagnosed with ADHD and loaded up with legal cocaine when he was about ten. That's when he started to label himself as a problem instead of as a person. Not as quirky or energetic but as ADHD. He started to believe he couldn't fit in. He lost his interest in theater and in anything athletic, then retreated into games. Only games.

Joey was seeing an excellent therapist, but the therapy wasn't helping. His parents and therapist brought him to me, and he was full of piss and vinegar, desperate to change. He said, "It's do or die." But then he'd yank up one eyebrow insanely high and sneak in something like, "But I'm not that bad."

As I started to discuss Joey with his parents, I suggested

that there was an iceberg under the water with Joey. I don't remember what exact advice or suggestion I offered, but his mother looked taken aback.

"Joey's basically normal," she insisted. "He works in my business, he's in school. He's not like some basket case."

I didn't bother to question her notion of Joey's "work" or "studying." I understood. The problem was, Joey wasn't burning down the house.

Drug addicts get into verbal and physical fights with their parents. They'll threaten their parents and others, get arrested, steal, pass out. If a mother says to her drug-abusing son, "You have to stop smoking marijuana in the house because of the other kids in the house," the drug addict will say, "Shut the fuck up, get the hell out of my face, you cunt" and stare her down menacingly. By the time parents come to me with their addict son, I know they've had enough. They are usually ready for change and the sacrifices that go along with it.

In contrast, the electronics guy, he just sits in his room and plays video games. The house isn't in an uproar. It's calm. The only reason the atmosphere is calmer with the electronics addict, as opposed to the drug addict, is because the parents are giving him what he wants. They know this behavior isn't normal but they don't want to force the issue.

"Would you consider taking away his electronics?" I asked his parents.

They looked at me as if it was the most bizarre question they'd ever heard. His mother slowly shook her head. "I would hope it wouldn't come to that," she said quietly. "You can't take away the only thing he has. Let's try other approaches."

I think they had a pretty clear idea of what Joey would do if they took away his electronics, even for a single hour. He'd throw chairs and TVs. He'd get physical.

She loved him. She loved him too much.

So, Joey and I began to meet. He knew his behavior wasn't normal. He admitted that gaming was a temporary and inadequate "solution" for connection, and that if he didn't learn to truly connect, he would remain unhappy in life. He was even a little savvy to some of his personal exits, the trapdoors in his mind. He arrived full of motivation. But motivation levels fluctuate, especially when things get difficult. You can't bank on them.

Pretty soon, he was questioning everything. "You are a therapist. That is how I see you. I don't want to connect to you. That is not going to change!"

Well, that was funny. Wasn't connection the very issue that had brought him in? Our time together would be a great laboratory where he could learn to connect. Slowly, we started to make small progress through that barrier.

Then new reasons emerged: "You're extroverted. We have nothing in common."

Then another reason: "You used spiritual language last time. I'm not spiritual, I'm a skeptic!"

He was trying to wriggle out of treatment.

Only a few weeks earlier he was "gung-ho." He understood the goal and the process. He promised he wouldn't back down. What happened? Well, we make promises until we feel the weight of those promises.

I tried to scare him a little. A woman in her thirties begins to biologically sense the need to settle down and give birth to a child. In that same way, men in their twenties feel the need to give birth to their life. I have never met a man in his twenties who hasn't felt that way. Addicts feel it, too, even if dimly. I told Joey that in terms of personal change, his window of opportunity would stay open until 30. After that, almost all men close down.

"You're losing your chance to change," I told him.

Joey deflected me. "It's not that bad. I'm working. I'm in school."

Yeah. He was a student. He could tell himself he was okay. People fool themselves on that for years.

"You're not that bad yet," I said. "But it's only a matter of time."

Meanwhile, his parents presented as empathic and very reasonable, but they empathized too much with their son, to the point that they couldn't tolerate seeing him suffer. But he needed to suffer. How was he going to grow and learn if he wasn't struggling and striving?

In one of our last conversations, I said, "Mrs. Feder, how is your son going to grow if he is not allowed to suffer at all? I see a clear pattern here: whenever Joey starts to suffer, you and your husband step in and bail him out. I need you to step back and let him suffer."

She nodded, agreeing. It seemed she was seeing through the fog.

"So what do I do?" she asked.

"Take away his electronics."

She seemed to reconsider this — for a second. "But what happens if he escalates?"

"You can absolutely guarantee that he is going to test you, greatly! Be prepared."

I saw panic in her eyes. Speaking to parents in this situation is like speaking to a kid standing at the edge of the diving board. No matter how many ways I say it, no matter how many times they get coached and resolve that they are going to do it, it comes down to a simple equation:

they either trust and jump, or they freeze in fear and stay.

It was way too scary for them to force the issue, to dispel the calm, even if it was an illusory calm. It would smash their illusion that Joey was normal, calm, nice. By forcing the issue, they would meet their son, and themselves. It would cause too much suffering for the parents.

Three days after our conversation, Joey dropped out of treatment with me.

After Joey, I realized something: there's a sweet spot. If the young man coming to me isn't badly damaged, I won't work with him. Because he and his parents are not convinced that it's desperation time. The clients who aren't so bad off, they talk such a good game but they always drop out after a month or two.

I still think of Joey, the way he could raise one brow really high, the outrageous face he made as if he'd eaten something sour. He was a big personality, and it was fun just to watch him exist. He must be almost thirty by now. I wonder if he ever graduated and got a real job, or maybe he's still going for a master's in something or nothing, so he and his parents can maintain the facade that he's okay, he's a student. I wonder if he has finally managed to ask a woman out, or even kiss her. I wonder if anyone has held the line for him. I wonder if anyone has held the line for him — and let him suffer.

Chapter 10

Connection is the Foundation

I f the line is held for young men, ultimately they will be faced with a simple fact: they do not know how to connect to other people in a way that is gratifying for them or others. That is what they are running from. So they retreat into themselves and wither in isolation, or else become takers, looking for things from others all the time. Sure, they are connecting in some way, but it is more of a superficial transaction instead of a deep connection.

* * *

Years ago, I was doing some in-home therapy with a seven-year-old boy. His home life was difficult — four siblings from multiple fathers who were hardly ever there. Each of the kids, particularly the boys, developed behavioral problems. The mother tried to keep it together by reaching out and finding resources, like this in-home therapy.

Oddly enough, the in-home method was very similar to the method I use today, at least in the sense that all the therapy took place in the environment where the person actually lives — their home and community — rather than an office.

The boy I was working with, Kevin, had a twin brother, who was also assigned a home therapist. Every time I picked Kevin up, I'd take him to the YMCA where we'd swim or play basketball. If it wasn't the Y, I'd take him to the park and then out for ice cream or pizza. He loved it when I came. It was his chance to get out of the house and go somewhere fun. When I showed up to get him each week, he would look straight past me to my car. It was his outlet, his chance to get out and have fun.

Once, we were sitting in my car outside the dollar store. I told him he could pick out some toy or whatever else he wanted, something that ordinarily excited him. Instead, Kevin just sat there, looking at his lap.

Obviously, something had happened. Each time he tried to tell me, he'd squeeze his eyes shut and shake his head. Eventually, the story came out: His father had stood him up for his birthday a few days ago. The tears he'd tried so hard to suppress finally came out.

Something between us shifted at that moment. It was only later that I realized the magnitude of what had happened. Kevin chose to stay in the car and tell me his story. He could've gone into the dollar store and picked out some toy. Instead, he chose to stay with me.

That was the energy shift I had experienced. I wasn't just the chauffeur to fun places. It shifted from him playing with me, to him really being with me. He had expanded his ability to be himself, and to connect, both to himself and someone else.

Unfortunately, my supervisor saw it differently. She called me into her office one day and reeled off all the amazing things the other therapist was doing with Kevin's twin brother (who was also getting in-home therapy through the organization): charts on the wall, working with rewards, behavior modification, DBT, CBT. The other therapist was doing all this cutting-edge cognitive stuff, and here I was, taking Kevin out for pizza. Now I had to face the tribunal. My heart was pumping. She ended nastily, "So, what have you been doing?"

Now that statement really lit a fire in me. Her words angered me so much that they galvanized me. I let loose a three-minute soliloquy about what I was doing and why. I spoke about the power of doing physical activities together, the power of exploring different places, the power of connecting. As I started to talk, I got into a rhythm.

"This whole universe exists through the power of connection. Think about it: social connections build communities, nations, and marriages. Connection is the foundation all the way down to chemical and atomic bonds.

"And no, my approach won't guarantee well-behaved choir boys, and that isn't even my aim. Building character and identity is my goal — because while behavior modification might produce a well-behaved kid, the same kid would act out as soon as the modification stopped. Those methods never penetrate, not really, into the core of a person's being. I am not looking to modify Kevin's behavior. I am looking to help Kevin learn the power of connection."

The room went silent.

"Oh," she said, smiling and backing off. "That's fantastic."

I had no idea at that time, but what I said encapsulated just about everything I would come to believe later in my career: that connection is the foundation of life, which is why it also needs to be the foundation of healing work.

I call it primal bonding. In essence, that's what I teach young men: how to connect. That's our aim, even when we are at our wit's end, like it was with Eddie.

Chapter 11

Eddie Would Go

Eddie came to me when he was two months shy of 18. I had never worked with that age group. Most kids at that age haven't sufficiently destroyed their lives yet — or the lives of everyone around them — at least not enough to convince their parents they need any outside form of intervention.

Eddie's biological parents were drug addicts. Up until five or six years old he grew up in a crack house. He remembered people coming into his house at all hours of the day and having sex in front of him. It's possible he was molested. At some point, the state took over, the parents lost custody, and Eddie got adopted by two kind people who devoted themselves to him and showed him love in the best way they knew how. They were older, in their late sixties.

Eddie was artistic and an excellent musician. He played guitar, piano, mandolin and was super-talented, but he affected a surfer-dude mentality, sort of shrugging off his talents and abilities. Yeah, I'm good at stuff. Whatever.

He was smart, talked the talk, acted mature beyond his years, and came up with insights about himself in the flat monotone he used when talking about his life. But I knew from his parents that he had episodes of extreme anger where he destroyed doors, walls, and chairs. He'd take off for days at a time without telling his parents where he was going. When he got really angry and couldn't leave, he'd physically threaten his parents. He called his mother the worst names in the book. Cunt, bitch, whore. He was so nasty to her. So angry.

The extreme and violent behavior had waned somewhat by the time Eddie got to me. When he was 16, his mother had taken a chunk of her life savings and sent him to an expensive six-month rehabilitation program in Arizona, a therapeutic school that stunted the destructive process in him. So Eddie wasn't that bad off by the time I met him, but he was still using drugs and refusing to follow home rules. You could feel the rage and violence simmering beneath his surfer-dude attitude. I thought of him as the Loch Ness Monster who'd come out from the lake, destroy things, and then go back under, not leaving a ripple, making you wonder if it had ever happened.

Our work began. We started with just basic hanging out, taking walks into town, going out for food or coffee. We did that for a few months. At times he did reduce his chemical intake, but it was only a periodic sobriety. He continued to straddle both worlds, which never works.

One day, we were sitting in a coffee shop, and he ordered himself something to eat. By then we'd been working together for eight months. There was a restlessness in the air. He fidgeted with the napkins, the sugar packets, his eyes darting everywhere except to me. I knew what was coming. The cordiality was about to dissolve between us. We'd had some tough interactions in the days prior, and Eddie was just not seeing any results from our work. Or not enough. He felt he'd made a lot of sacrifices. He couldn't get high like he used to with his friends. He had to give up some of his time to spend it with me, and he didn't want to do it anymore. His sacrifices hadn't proven their value in the months he'd invested with me.

My whole method rests on finding joy in life and in connecting. Of course, there is a process of searching, and I tell my guys we're all on this journey of seeking, but there has to be a process of finding, of reaching land. You can't always keep telling the guy, "keep going, keep going."

As he ate his donut and drank his coffee, I could feel

it in the air: the anger, the bleakness, the frustration, and this huge disconnect. A million thoughts flew through my mind.

I wanted to knock that stupid donut out of his hand. I wanted to shout at him, to wake him up. He needed to deepen this connection, not end it. I knew he wanted more, not less. He wanted to feel whole, alive, connected, awestruck and wonderful. He wanted to feel his own agency and power, even if he couldn't articulate it. Is it any wonder why he used chemicals to alter his state of mind? People want connection — need it, crave it — but when they can't get it, they stomp on that desire. It doesn't matter, Eddie might say back.

I nearly told him, "You are stupid enough to think that you are all-powerful and free, because you can end relationships, because you can end life. Man, you are so terrified of losing this scrap of connection that you have to get there first and do the leaving yourself. I wonder if even you are fooled. Don't try to enlist me to aid your self-sabotage and destruction!"

He wouldn't have understood. He would've just said, "This is who I am."

"No," I might've replied. "This is who you have become."

I wanted to tell him to keep going, but I'd already demanded that from him for the past eight months.

Instead, I sat quietly with him while he ate, all while taking stock of the feelings ping-ponging inside me.

Finally, I said to Eddie, "Why don't you come up with one new thing we could try together?"

He thought for a long moment. He let out a sigh, as if telling himself, one more week, and then I'll make my getaway.

"Well, I always wanted to try rock climbing," he said. "There's a rock-climbing gym near my town."

So that's where we went.

When I was climbing the wall, Eddie needed to keep the rope taut so I wouldn't fall, and if Eddie was climbing, it was my job to be his eyes, to let him know, from my angle, what was the next move to make. Go left, now go right. Put your right arm a little higher, at two o'clock. Yep, you've got it. Now put your left foot on the toehold.

We each took turns supporting the other. Each rock was another exercise in problem solving. Where do I shift my body weight, how far can I stretch without losing my balance? Rock by rock, we were not only climbing the wall before us; we were two men climbing the wall between us, building trust *between* each other and in our own bodies and selves. Neither of us would've died if we had messed up, because there's an emergency auto-belay device that catches you at the last second. But you still need trust for that — that the back-up will work!

Eddie was experiencing, in his body and muscles and joints, how the path upward requires patience and persistence, that it's full of twists and unexpected turns. And all that's needed is to make it to the next rock.

His rock-climbing idea saved everything. After a few months of doing that, we started going to New York City. He discovered really high-end tattoo parlors, and we went to check out their work. We'd go out to eat and shop at the bohemian thrift shops in The Village. He loved getting quality clothing at bargain prices. We were having really great experiences together.

During that time, he developed his first relationship with a girl. It helped him mature a little bit when he saw his issues play out in relation to her. It became harder for him to place all his problems at his parents' feet.

Once, I went with him and his girlfriend to pick out his tuxedo for the prom. During that experience, I became a part of their world. I wasn't some outside presence. He'd try on a tux, and me and his girlfriend would laugh and shake our heads. The next tux looked better, and we gave him the thumbs up. Finally, he'd narrowed it down to two, and he chose the one he wanted. I could see the pure happiness on his face.

Here was an 18-year-old kid with his sweetheart, and they were looking for a tux for the prom. I could see the innocence and the love. He wasn't stuck in his room, gaming, jerking off, smoking weed, and eating three-day-old pizza. He was where he was supposed to be. Every young man longs to be doing that — no matter if they say otherwise.

Eddie had earned his prom experience. It wasn't a matter of some guy taking a shower, sprucing himself up, hiring some escort and going out to rent a tux. It took a lot of effort and sacrifice to get to that point. He sacrificed getting high with his friends. He relinquished time — and control of his life to a degree — because he had to be with me sometimes. He had to give up giving up, which may have been hardest of all.

And he needed this resolve, because through all of this, it wasn't easy. Stuff comes up when you are truly doing the dirty work of connecting to life and to another human being.

One time, I made a comment that bothered him. It was insensitive, and I apologized.

Eddie persisted, "You should know that it bothers me. You said the same thing last month too, and I keep telling you it bothers me!"

Yeah, he was right. I had said something that offended him and I should've known better, been more careful. But something in his tone was saying, "This is a sore spot for me, so the rest of the world better avoid it." It reeked to me of victim mentality.

I knew this attitude carried over into his relationships not only with me but with his family, his friends, and girlfriend. Of course, I needed to take responsibility for my mistakes and my own triggers. If I didn't do that, I couldn't ask or model for Eddie how to do it.

What I ultimately wanted to teach Eddie, and what he was able to learn, was how to stay in the conflict and allow it to resolve. He and I rolled so many times through that process that it became second nature. And each time he did, he was able to tap into a deeper part of himself, to grow, and in the end, to connect and love. And so was I.

Other men do the exact opposite. Because they are resistant to the deeper work, they end up leaving each of their relationships. They dream of true connection but are afraid of it. In the end, these men think of themselves as "powerful" and "free" by virtue of leaving their relationships, by leaving their reality.

Eddie and I worked together for over two years. Today, Eddie has made so much of himself. He is definitely not perfect, but he's in tune with his journey and trying to become a better human being. He strives to be worldly yet humble, self-aware and self-reliant, and the creator of a life that he enjoys.

We still keep in touch. The last time we met, we ate at the coffee shop he works at, one of his two jobs. His coworkers knew who I was and watched us fondly as we spent time laughing, recalling all the good memories, and all the challenges we went through together. Everyone longs for this type of connection, one built though years of hard work, ups and downs.

Years ago, I heard the story of Eddie Aikau, a Hawaiian surfer who became legendary for surfing big waves and for acting as a lifeguard, paddling out in the most treacherous conditions to save a fallen surfer. His ability to brave all elements led to a local slogan when facing extreme adversity: Eddie would go.

I thought of that story when I looked at my client. Who would've thought that Eddie, with his crazy childhood past, would've developed the ability to sit through the hard stuff in a relationship and in life and stay committed . . . no matter what.

Chapter 12

Get a Job

I saw the power of staying the course — no matter what — in relationships and in all endeavors in life. But there seemed to be some sort of barrier that prevented young men from making firm commitments. I needed a way to teach them to engage with life, not only at the relational and explorational levels. I wanted them to plant a flag in the ground, and to make firm choices for their lives. I needed some sort of threshold.

Dan and I had been walking together for a while. He'd been getting to know me, and I was getting to know him. We had a bond, a relationship. We'd also explored the town and its surroundings, and tried out different activities. He was athletic, and we both loved playing sports together. Important progress had been made, but was our process complete? I sensed there was a next stage.

There was something about Dan that didn't strike me as quite right. If you looked at him, he was this big, good-looking, young man. He was muscular and moved around with ease. He was bright too. I enjoyed his observations about culture or all the different types of music he was into. It would be hard to see that not too long ago he was deeply addicted to drugs, his mind crumbling along with his life.

But he had managed to give all that up. And yet, while his life should have been improving, it really wasn't. The more time I spent with him, the more I sensed how clueless and rootless he felt.

Working with me, he started to make progress. Yes, he was willing to venture out and try an art class or squash, a sport he had never tried before. But everything he did was subject to his whims and feelings. If he didn't feel like doing something, he would cancel or cut it short without much thought. When the art exhibit was kind of boring, he would bail. On rainy and windy days, he thought, why bother leaving the house to go see the show we got tickets for? Something about this didn't sit right with me. This sturdy, muscular guy was actually floating in the wind. He needed to be able to really sink his teeth into something. He needed to engage.

So, what would the engagement step for Dan look like? It would start by making a commitment to something that he would have to do, whether or not he liked it or felt good that day.

We started by trying to commit to a specific hobby, like a style of hot yoga, or work toward a particular goal with weightlifting like being able to bench 300 pounds. But Dan was still lackadaisical, flighty. He didn't want to tie himself down to anything.

Watching Dan float around, I realized something. By not engaging, Dan felt all options were open to him. Choosing one project, one path, one apartment, one woman, was a kind of death for him.

And to a degree, Dan was right. If he chose one career, for instance, it meant closing himself off to another path. By not choosing and opting for the do-nothing way, he could remain in a limbo land of eternal possibility. He could con himself into thinking he had all the power and was always free to walk away. Decision involves incision, because to arrive at a single point of action, other avenues must be cut off.

But there was another side to Dan: the hungry side, the part that longed to do something, to make something, to feel that creative energy and to be breathing that energy into life. But how could he take that longing and make it a reality? How could he make something stick deeper and for more than an hour?

One day, Dan and I had lunch at a restaurant. We were outside, and I was taking in the nice sunshine. The wait staff were all young and wore nicely ironed shirts and pants. I watched as they swiftly carried platters of food and drinks. No one was bumping into each other. They were coordinated and in harmony with one another. It almost looked like a symphony.

And they were not thinking of themselves. One waiter brought crayons to some kids so they could draw and give their parents a break. A nearby couple asked their waiter what dessert they should order. "Our marble cheesecake is the best!" he said proudly, as if he had made it himself.

In contrast, Dan was lounging in his khakis and flip flops. He was looking down at his plate and shoveling food into his mouth. I noticed that even though he was enjoying himself, he wasn't as deeply involved with the whole performance. In other words, if Shakespeare was right that "all the world's a stage, and all the men and women, merely players," then Dan had a very small and insignificant role. He eats, he pays, he leaves. Yes, his life was comfortable but also flat. In essence, he was missing out on all the ups and downs of life, and everything in between. He gave me the impression of a huge tiger in a zoo: waking, having his lunch brought to him, taking a stroll around the cage, gazing indifferently at the people taking an interest in him, then settling down for an afternoon nap. The poor tiger had no idea there was a vibrant, exciting jungle out there, and that he had a place in it.

In that moment, I thought of something the eminent depth psychologist Carl Jung once said. Someone asked him what could be done about what was then called Peter Pan Syndrome — boys who don't grow up. He replied, "Only one thing. Work."

Of course!

Getting a job is just so basic. It's one of the fundamental tasks of a man. And what a perfect way to demonstrate engagement, because when a young man takes a job, he moves from tourist to citizen. Now he has a part in the play. He is not an observer; he is now a participant.

I pushed aside my bowl of ramen. "Dan, I think it's time we help you get a job."

"Yeah, sounds cool," he said with a shrug.

He didn't sound as committed to the idea as I would've liked, but it was a start.

We began by looking on job websites. His interest was piqued, but our ideas about his qualifications were worlds apart. Dan started listing professional jobs that were high-paying and required great responsibility. He said he could work for Apple or Google or some tech company. He was a smart kid, so it made some sense that he wanted to use his abilities.

We looked at his resume. Four years ago, he was a camp counselor for a month. Two years ago, he worked for a political campaign for a few months. I saw a lot of academic and personal attributes, but as the saying goes, "You can't bullshit a bullshitter." There was virtually no work experience

"Uh, Dan . . . Why do you think you can get a job working at Google?"

He looked puzzled by my question.

"Hey, I know I can work that job," he said and rolled his eyes as if even Google was beneath him.

Man, he had no idea what job he was capable of. Some part of me wanted to just shove reality in his face, tell him how totally delusional he was. Instead, I figured I'd let reality do its work for me.

We spent the next few weeks poring over and applying for jobs. And yes, the rejections piled up. But still, as the reality was hitting Dan, the rejections mostly led to excuses and blame.

"It's the bad economy. It's too many immigrants. Everyone's got a thing these days against white men or black men, or tall men. This job wouldn't have challenged me anyway."

I was struggling to find a way to break through his faulty thinking. One day, I asked Dan to come up with some of the easiest jobs he could think of.

He thought a second. "I don't know. A garbage man, a dishwasher, a janitor."

Hmm. A janitor. A lightbulb went off in my head. That's perfect. I found an ad with a custodian's job requirement and duties. I waited a week and then showed the job description to Dan:

- Perform routine inspection and maintenance activities
- Notify management of deficiencies or needs for repairs
- Make adjustments and minor repairs
- Stock and maintain supply rooms
- Clean and supply designated building areas
- Cooperate and work as part of a team and independently
- Carry out heavy cleaning tasks and special projects
- Follow all health and safety regulations and requirements

"Do you think you could fulfill this job description?" I asked.

He scanned the list of duties. "Whoa. I don't know," he said. "It sounds . . . kind of involved. Complicated stuff."

Damn right, I thought.

"Dan, it's a position to be a janitor."

Dan squinted his eyes. Was he angry? Or defeated? I couldn't tell.

"Do you think you can do it? Can you clean and stock a room?" I asked, pointing to his kitchen.

There were vape cartridges strewn over the counter, empty boxes of to-go food all over the table, an empty refrigerator, no dish soap.

Dan's face fell. Now he looked angry. He thought he was ready for greatness, for running the New York Yankees in a corner office with windows overlooking Central Park. And here he was seeing that he wasn't qualified to be a janitor, which is a great job by the way!

Dan deflated right before my eyes. "You're telling me I can't even be a lousy janitor?!"

I told him that the list of duties proved there is no such thing as a lousy janitor, that it required a whole array of skills that were probably beyond him. He sulked and moaned for days after that.

Hey you, my man reading this book. How about you? How do you react when your mom asks you to replace toilet paper or take out garbage, or when your dad asks you to help mow the lawn? When was the last time you looked at your parents and said, hey guys, I noticed we are low on laundry detergent. I'll go pick some up. What's your level of integrity and initiative?

After Dan got over his self-importance, he had to tackle his self-pity, which was just the other side of that coin. First, he thought he was the alpha dog. Now he thought he was dog shit. Neither was true.

"Dan," I said, "has anyone like your dad ever sat you down and showed you how to get a job?"

He thought about it a little, then shook his head.

I said, "The first rule is that getting a job is your job."

He was listening.

"Rule two: Clean up your resume. If your resume was a confession, you'd be going to hell! The good news is the world is forgiving."

Dan agreed to take a course on how to write a resume and cover letter.

"Rule three: You need to devote serious blocks of time to this. It's your job, remember? Rule four: Don't do it alone. Have someone, preferably a man, guide you."

Thankfully, he rolled up his sleeves and began to work with me. It took him about three weeks to get his resume in shape. Then another two weeks to learn the art of the follow-up with an email or phone call.

Finally, after five weeks he got his first interview, then another after that. Dan was still so resistant to following up. After live meetings, he made excuses: "I didn't get a great feeling about that place." "The boss looked at me weird." "I bombed that one." "I don't think they were interested in me at all." "I don't want to waste my time calling them back."

Every time we met, he would rattle off those excuses. Dan started following up with every place he went to, but the process continued for weeks. I sensed Dan was getting defeated. He worked hard not to get stuck in feelings of rejection.

I'll never forget the day he finally got a job. One moment we were walking across the street to follow up in-person with a place he had applied to a week ago. The next moment he was walking out of the place with a smile on his face.

The sun was out that day. Dan walked proudly. He felt so good about himself. He got the job. Not me. Not his dad, not his dad's friend. It was a job at the front desk of a local gym. Even though he wasn't totally qualified, the manager liked him and wanted to give him a chance. He would have to greet customers, take phone calls, clean areas. It was part-time but with opportunity to advance. They even planted a seed that one day Dan might work his way up to personal training. He was seeing the pieces of the puzzle coming together, but it would not be easy. He was the morning shift, so he would have to get up early — each day, no excuses. That meant no staying up late and watching stupid videos or playing games.

Whereas exploration is trying things and putting out feelers, I see engagement as choosing to commit to something. Emerging men struggle with that commitment. They feel there are too many setbacks, defeats, detours. The escapisms and excuses start, and that derails the whole process. Fortunately, there is a trick that has the power to get them on track . . . and stay on track.

Chapter 13

Primal Storytelling

When I first met Doug, he began to tell me his story. "In kindergarten, I was held back a year. In second grade, my parents divorced. When I was nine, I got diagnosed as ADHD. Later, in my teens, we realized I was borderline."

He must have recited this many times before, because he reeled it off with almost no feeling. He had every detail down pat. As I listened, I was both amazed and bored. This is what he calls his life story? A case history, yes. A life story, it was not.

There is something terribly sad when not only the listener is bored, but the teller has no interest in his own story. Instead of talking leading to insight, breakthrough and change, here the talking was actually serving as a barrier to progress. I nearly said, "That's a shopping list of diagnoses, not a story!"

Instead of giving your case history, you might do what the mythologist Martin Shaw recommends: mythologize your pathologies. Put your problems and challenges within the context of a myth, a deeper story that has purpose, a life, a heart. One of the greatest features of storytelling is that it places people in the context of a living myth. Then they become a hero in their own story. To do that, you need to choose how to see the story you are living in.

I once heard a story that John F. Kennedy was walking through the NASA building during the space race when the U.S. was trying to launch to the moon. The tour was mostly ceremonious, with the president getting a look at the inside of the operation and meeting and greeting people involved.

As JFK was walking through the hallway, there was a man cleaning the floors in the hallway with great care. His energy was so noticeable that the president paused and greeted the man.

"So, what is it that you do here?"

"Well, Mr. President," he said with a beaming smile, "I'm helping to put a man on the moon."

There is an art of telling a story, your story, in a way that positions it in an intriguing, compelling way — a way that makes people, including yourself, interested in what will happen. It's another tool I use when trying to lead people toward a deeper involvement with something outside themselves. It's a very powerful tool, especially for men.

Imagine your life as if it were a series on Netflix. Would you tune in every week to watch it? Would you want to binge the whole season? Would anyone else be interested? If the answer is no, then it's a sign that you're stagnating and need to make some major changes. If you yourself would not be interested in watching your own life play out on television, that is a red flag that you are not really engaged with your life. You need to be invested in your story in order to guide it, shape it, and to make it happen. If the way you are telling your story does not capture your imagination and passion, then you will simply not muster the power to enter it and live in it in a creative and goal-oriented way.

Add some new characters and start to shake things up and try different activities. Start to get a sense of what the story of your life is about. Tell the real story of your life, not a boring episodic one with no deeper theme or running plot. Who is the hero trying to become? What is his goal? What obstacles are getting in his way? Tell the story where you are the hero, setting out on a difficult journey, who sometimes wins but also gets knocked down at times. He keeps getting up, keeps his vision fixed on his goal.

With Doug, I kept reframing his life in a way that I sensed could actually excite him, so that he was living an open-ended myth, instead of a closed, limited death sentence.

"Doug, how is it going with your journey of learning to sincerely love yourself and others?" I would ask when he started bombarding me and the group with his diagnoses about how he is personality disordered and how that's the reason he cannot feel genuine concern.

I don't want you to think that we are talking about some Arthurian Tale, slaying dragons and rescuing beautiful women. The myth is usually not in the clouds, but rather right here in reality.

Take the NASA janitor — let's call him Brad — for instance. Yes, he sees his work as part of a larger story, and that's amazing. He sees that his keeping physical order at NASA, in its own way, is getting a man on the moon. And it is. Happiness, for him, is being able to go to work and get satisfaction from what he does. It is not just about the money — it is about a different type of currency, an unseen energy Brad gives and receives from life.

But the road to finding and maintaining that outlook is a daily, if not hourly, challenge. First, he has to get over the fact that people's eyes glaze over when they see him — if they see him at all. Mostly he's invisible to others.

The world out there drums it into our heads — get ahead, make more, have more, at whatever cost, be it psychic, emotional, or moral. It's the religion of America. Brad's struggle, even if it's below the surface, is to not side with his detractors. It's to always be visible — to himself and to his personal mission.

Well, you might say, is it really that hard? After all, Brad has his own bunch of friends and co-workers to hang around with and validate him. But that's not the case here. Brad's pal Rick who is in charge of setting up and maintaining the conference rooms is always complaining about the last meeting or party, the board of directors who stank up the room with their cigarettes, the astronauts who dropped their empty snack bags wherever they felt like, scattering crumbs all over the table and floor, like some untrained toddlers. Underneath the complaints, Rick is seething with the bitterness of what he perceives as a small life. Every day, Brad has to resist getting sucked into Rick's toxic negativity. So, how does he steer clear of that?

And how does he keep his mind from exploding from boredom? Every day, he deals with the same or slightly different messes, cleaning up other people's careless garbage and the toilets other people use. Not only is his work never done, it is constantly undone. To be repeated the next day.

Talk about Sisyphean! And yet Brad finds a way to find the joy in his work.

Finding joy in work — any work — is a challenge. In fact, it is *the* challenge. Most of the men I work with believe they can only find joy in work when they have "the job of their dreams."

Brad is privy to a secret. He knows that whatever you do in life, whether it's a school principal, astronaut, vegetable cutter, or manager of a laundromat, your work can be shoddy, mediocre, or excellent. In every task lies a seed of greatness, true excellence. He understands that his life is an unfolding story, with twists and turns and daily battles that are exciting to him even if they aren't visible to others. He's not a saint, but he's not a machine either. He doesn't win them all, obviously, or they wouldn't pose a true challenge. He handles all the battles that come up in his work, in his life story, with utmost integrity. These battles are an integral part of the process. It is at these moments of challenge that most of us want to give up and throw in the towel. It is at these moments when we find all types of excuses to give up, when instead we could mythologize and keep going.

* * *

Nick landed a great job as a salesman at a video game store. He had such a passion and knowledge for video games that he excelled and was promoted twice within a year. Before he knew it, he was offered the position of store manager at a different location. Now Nick was faced with a hard decision. He was very happy in his present role at the store, and the new store did have potential drawbacks. I really admired the way he considered the options, spoke with others, and processed through the decision. He finally decided to take the position at the new store. He was pleased and felt good.

Two weeks later, Nick dropped by.

"Hey, how's it going?" I asked.

"I hate my job — I hate everything about it."

"Why? What's the problem?"

"For one, it's a store within a department store, so the selection of games blows. Also, my old job had younger customers, all buying games I know about. These customers are all old people buying stupid games for their kids."

Nick resolved to stick it out a bit, but before he even got a chance to get his feet wet, the store fell into a bad slump. The upper management laid all the blame on Nick. Nick was bitter and angry.

"Now the leadership views me as a loser!" Nick continued.

"So they are 'wrongly' blaming you for the store's troubles and you hate that," I said.

Nick nodded emphatically.

I stared at him as he cracked his knuckles, his big-muscled shoulders hunched. Even in his white-collar shirt, he looked like the athlete he once was. And to an athlete, there is nothing better than making a comeback.

I said, "Then I guess you have the chance to make this a comeback story. Everyone loves a comeback story."

Man, did his eyes light up! Because now he was at the center of a tale, a myth. Seeing his life as a story gave Nick the ability to stay and weather the blows, to recommit to the job, and to see it through to the end. Now Nick had a chance to take charge of the story, his story. He could choose whether to argue over who was right or wrong, or to accept the situation and use all his creative power to improve the store. He had the power to choose whether he was sweeping the floor or helping put a man on the moon. He had a chance to become a hero.

Chapter 14

The Male Womb

Years ago, when I started this work, I figured out a few things in short order. First, I needed to bring my guy out of the office. It's a basic idea, but for me it was transformative. I also needed to either be his mentor or find him a mentor, help him find a path in life that would teach him through lessons rather than just words. I needed to actively challenge him and help activate his survival instinct. All good and necessary tools.

But at some point, I had to ask myself: Where were we going with these tools? What was the aim? Tools are great, but only if you know what they are working toward.

At first, my intuition fueled my work. Later, I had the vision: The aim was moving from being a helpless, deeply frustrated and confused boy to becoming a creative, powerful, and loving man.

I saw this change happening in four stages: bonding, exploring, engaging, and ultimately, creating. These stages wouldn't be static, as in: "Okay, I've bonded enough, now let me go out and get to the exciting stuff, the creation stage." Instead, they would be forever ongoing, like a river, one stream forever flowing into the next, each one replenishing the other.

I envisioned these rivers flowing into the heart of the male, an eternal, easy flow, with no force. These streams would irrigate his heart, keep his valves clean and fresh and vital.

These are the stages we went through together: Bonding. Exploring. Engaging. Creating.

At least that's how I termed them. That was my vision, for my guys and for myself. Having this template helped me understand where a young man might be getting stuck and how to help him become what I knew he was destined to become — a creator.

* * *

Ever notice how in ancient cultures there are so many male initiation rites? Even today, some of these practices still exist, rituals for boys becoming men, most of them full of pomp and pageantry. Societies have to come up with these male rites of passage, which often seem puny when compared to the natural rites of passage women experience.

The moment a woman has a child, she has crossed a clear and defined threshold deeper into the feminine. She has become a creator; she feels she's sharing the stage with God in bringing a brand new human being into the world. Of course, she creates in countless other ways, too, but ask any mother and she'll tell you that was a defining moment.

Men, on the other hand, lack a clear threshold of crossing into masculinity. Without this clear way of reaching our depths and our purpose, we men feel a void. And we experience that void like a gaping wound. Is it any wonder we men stuff ourselves with things like cars, women, titles, and chemicals?

But guess what? The inner void isn't the problem. It's what you fill it with that becomes the issue.

In one scientific study, spiders were given different chemicals: psychedelics, alcohol, and cocaine. Their webs were then compared to sober spiders. The results spoke volumes: the intoxicated spiders' webs made no damn sense! They lacked the symmetry, wholeness and purpose of their sober buddies. What does this tell you? Put drugs into animals and their planning capacities go haywire.

Having the advantage of closely witnessing other men's lives, I can see that the problem isn't simply that men are using chemicals. The drugs are just a symptom of the real problem. In fact, I see that the use of chemicals and the entire lifestyle is really an attempt to fill a void within.

One day, while putting an event together, I was talking to the event's musician and pondering questions I could ask the group. During this contemplation, I felt an odd sensation and had a eureka moment. The inner void is the male womb. That void and sense of emptiness is a purposeful part of us. It's the place from where men build cities and bridges, create events, invent cars, and make marriages and families.

It is a divine hunger inside us. The man who wastes that hunger on distractions — stuffing himself with cars, drugs, a new Rolex, high-paying jobs — engorges himself on all the bright lights of the world. Still, he will feel empty. None of these things are inherently bad or wrong, but ultimately men need a dream, not a distraction.

But we are distracted, and our culture is only encouraging us to be more so. The prevailing view is that this void is something bad that needs to be fixed ASAP.

"I feel lonely. I am so angry. I feel lost," our young men think. Society responds in kind: Take medication quick! Leave the relationship — or fix the relationship —

now! Watch a movie or a show and get filled on someone else's life. Today's culture is offering cheap and misguided fixes that essentially keep us going the wrong way, instead of tackling the core issue.

What if instead of this fruitless and pointless outward search, we instead tell men that they were born to be creators, and that creation is an actual place inside their male psyche?

Creation is the place where every man wants to arrive. And by creation I mean having an idea that excites them, whether that is an idea for an app, or a business they are developing, or a relationship they are building. Men have an image, a desire in their being, and they are putting effort and energy toward manifesting that desire. That process is called creation.

What if we warned men that if they don't find this place within, the consequences are worse than failing to find water and food? In a desperate attempt to access their own womb, men often try aggressively to inflict their own limited form of power onto the world. Sometimes the attempts are weak and pathetic; other times they are wantonly violent and cause great damage and pain.

Doesn't this sound like what we are seeing in men these days, especially young men? Look around. Anyone can see that the numbers of men suffering from drug addiction, violence, incarceration, suicide, are staggering compared to those statistics for women.

Parents endlessly plead with their sons (and ultimately with me) about how much more their sons could be accomplishing. They could have a job. They could be doing better in school. They could have more direction in life. They could be happier. Yeah, they could be creators.

When I work with young men and I see their intense frustration, destructiveness, and self-destruction, I know it is because these creators are getting defeated in the process of creating.

Remember Nick, the one whose company brass blamed him for the program's failure right after he took it over? Nick was livid, seething. He was getting ready to lash out. That's when Nick and others need to be firm, and remind themselves of their deeper goal, of what they want to create.

"Nick! You already knew there were problems here! You yourself tried to tell management about those problems! You took this job because you wanted to build a great store. So, what's changed?"

Once Nick got off the ledge, he saw that all his feelings were just obstacles to his creative force, hurdles that if used properly could actually deepen and intensify the creative drive.

It's helpful to define your feelings in these terms: "I am a Creator who is getting frustrated or feeling hopeless or overwhelmed in the process of creating."

Ron was in his mid 20s and feeling fed up from going from job to job and relationship to relationship. He was despondent because he hadn't made anything of his life. He didn't care much about bonding or exploring or engaging, but Ron did want to build something concrete, something he could be proud of and call his own.

He didn't really care at all about bonding, or exploring, or engaging, which was no surprise. If you were to stop any man on the street and ask him if bonding or connection with others or committing is up high on his agenda, he'd probably say no. But Ron did want to build something concrete, something he could be proud of and call his own.

When Ron and I started to focus on what he would like to create and put all our efforts into that, he came up with an idea: he and his friends wanted to start an eBay company that sold quick-sale products. He and his buddies started meeting every week to discuss their idea. They created to-do lists, had one of their mom's design the logo, and joined an online circle that helps people build online platforms. As they started to create, I saw the fire growing in Ron. That fire is the medicine. It actually ended up cooking off some of the fat everyone wanted gone, like

Ron's laziness, depression, drug use, isolation, and video games. For him and other men, *creation is the solution.*

My friend, let me share with you something that almost killed me to learn: The void is not bad. It's good. It was put inside you to help you build worlds.

So, the next time you feel that dull aching emptiness in you, don't rush to binge on food or entertainment or some chemical. Instead, have an encounter with the void. Ask yourself questions like: What is this fix distracting me from? What is my soul demanding of my life? What would make me truly happy and fulfilled? Let yourself be surprised!

You, brother, were born to create.

Chapter 15

The Great Catalyst

Using the primal tools, I helped pave a path for the young men I was working with. They were reaching states of independence and happiness.

Throughout this process, though, I realized there was a hidden power that made this all possible: I was on the journey with them. I was changing. I was growing. I was leading the way.

The great catalyst in this process seemed to be my own story, which continued throughout my journey alongside the men I accompanied. I discovered that the key with the mentor's impact is that you can only take them as far as you yourself have gone.

So, how far have I gone?

Well, my journey has taken me almost twenty-five years of daily work to clarify and correct the patterns that nearly destroyed me, and to repair the damage they caused myself and others. Sometimes I feel I have "made it," and other times I feel that I've gone nowhere.

Recently, while discussing this with my friend and colleague, I told him, "I don't know if I have made it anywhere at all."

He seemed to understand my sentiment. He looked deeply at me and replied with his lovely British accent: "But you've gone far."

I feel that to be true.

PART TWO

MY PRIMAL STORY

Chapter 16

Crazy Train

I wasn't ever sleeping easily. Any sleep I did get was a thin slice sandwiched between fear and dread. Constant worry kept me in a state of angst. How will I make money to pay off my gambling debts? Where would I get my next drug to soothe myself? Had my dorm neighbor figured out it was me who had stolen his computer, on which he'd saved a semester's worth of research? I overheard my football coaches discuss me, saying, "What the hell is he doing?" That must've been the time I rode my motorcycle for hours all night and showed up late for the football game the next day. I walked into the locker room exhausted and disheveled, my eyes half-closed and my hair a mess as my team waited, already dressed in uniform, ready to walk out for the start of the game. I was benched. It was a big game, too.

My body was in decline. I was having excruciating back pain and could barely move. The pain shot down through my legs, and I was unable to touch even my chin to my chest. Just to play football I had to get very painful therapy treatments called point stimulation. I completely understand why they are no longer used. Every day the therapist would point a device at my lower back that looked like a cow prong with two large metal hooks. It was supposed to loosen the tissue there, but the only real benefit was that the pain it produced distracted me from my injury's pain. I played for the entire season, despite being debilitated during the weekdays between games.

Midway through the semester, I placed an innocent bet on a football game. Two weeks later, I was up $4,000. The bookie told me to wait until next weekend to get my pay out. I agreed, and by next weekend I went from plus $4,000 to minus $1,000. By the end of the semester, I had lost close to $30,000.

One day, my mother came up to college to visit me. We sat, ironically, at Mother's Tavern. She looked at me pleadingly with deep concern and asked me why I was sniffing and twitching so much. There was no way I would admit to her I was sniffing because I was snorting drugs. I deflected and assured her I was okay, just under the weather. What I didn't know was that she'd gone home that night and told my father that she thought I was going to die.

I was a bullet train speeding through life, but with no idea where I was going and with little control of the locomotive. I did know from my upbringing that I was going the wrong way, that all the things I was doing were not good. My father, a lapsed Greek Orthodox Christian, and my mother, a lapsed Jew, had never formally instructed me, but they were highly moral people, humble and devoted to family. My adult life was dissonant from my upbringing, but I kept moving farther away from that moral upbringing, faster and faster. The train was starting to feel like a runaway, heading on a collision course.

I sensed doom and was looking for a way out. One night, I woke up like a gunshot at 3 a.m. I rolled over on my small bed and looked out the dorm window. There was fierce yellow moonlight screaming into my room. I sat up in bed. I didn't know why I'd woken. I just felt some intensity, a vibration. I had gone to sleep in my usual state of panic and dread over my life, but that was normal for me.

I looked out the window again. The moon was exuding a raw energy. Buzzzzzz… It was at a different frequency than I was. I could've sworn it was right at my window, and it was imploring me to wake up. Wake up! Then I heard these words. *Move to Greece.* Those were actual words that I heard, alone in my room at 3 a.m.

Move to Greece? I'd probably been there six or seven times during summer breaks from school, visiting my father's family. It was certainly a part of my life, but I hadn't been there in a while. And never until that very moment did I even consider the thought of living there.

But now that I had it, Yes! I grabbed onto the idea as if I'd been given an answer to all my problems. I knew it was probably my only next move. I felt it. I had to move to Greece, no matter what.

When I told my family, my friends and football coaches, their reactions were not what I expected. Everyone was shocked and thought I was crazy! As the rejection and confusion from others mounted, part of me started to doubt myself. Was I insane, or visionary? My parents, my girlfriend, my football coaches — no one could understand. The only ones who understood were those traveling aboard that same runaway train: my friends.

A college buddy came to me one day and asked if he could come with me. He was as desperate and afraid as I was. As I looked at him, I felt sorry for him. Then again, he was one of the reasons I had to leave. I had to extricate myself from my peers and my life at the time. In my heart, I knew I needed to be finished with this chapter of my life, including everyone in it. So I said no. Leaving meant being alone.

On the night before I left for Greece, my mother came to my room as I packed. She was quietly crying. In her hand she held an index card. Without speaking, she handed it to me.

It was a poem and a personal note scrawled in red. I read the poem — it was about a mother's love and hope for her child. I looked back at my mother and smiled. She came to say good luck. I was her firstborn son, the difficult one who faced and created great trouble, the one she infused so much blood and belief into.

I quietly continued to pack my things, smiling, because I knew that I had my mother's blessing.

Chapter 17

Sisyphus's Boulder

I was sitting at the bottom of the stairs that led to my aunt's three-story apartment building at 11 Propileon in Athens, Greece. My father grew up in this same home; it has been in our family for almost fifty years.

Costa, a man in his 70s, arrived by taxi. He stepped out of the cab, dressed in a collared shirt and blue slacks which he wore like a uniform. Even in extreme heat, Greek men will never wear shorts. I greeted him with a smile and wave, and together we proceeded to climb the stairs, arm in arm.

This was the task given to me by my aunt Corinna: personally escort each elderly person up the winding stairs to the frequent dinners she hosted. Naturally, after dinner I ferried them back down, though this proved to be more difficult because by then they were tired and drunk.

Just a few weeks earlier, I had arrived in Greece knowing only a few Greek words and phrases: Hello, good-bye, cucumber, ice cream, I love you a lot, and all of the swear words my friends had taught me when I was young.

Now Costa was talking to me in Greek. I could tell by the tone that he was asking me questions. Didn't this guy know that I couldn't speak any Greek? It was so damn frustrating! In the end, I feigned a response with my head or shoulders. Costa looked at me confused, then gave up and lowered his head as we continued to trudge slowly up the stairs.

This would not change. All the old people I shepherded up and down these stairs were going to talk to me. The Greeks hate silence, and they hate admitting they need help even more. So they tried to make it seem like this adventure up the stairs was a formality rather than a necessity.

But it was absolutely necessary. There were no elevators in the building. The stairs, still concrete and unfinished, snaked dangerously and without a guardrail, spiraling around up to the third floor where my aunt and I lived. Anyone could easily fall while ascending and descending. The whole journey reminded me of the myth of Sisyphus, who was sentenced to an eternity of pushing a heavy boulder up a mountain, only to have it roll back down. Then he'd have to start over again.

Adding onto my own torture was the fact that I was still in a lot of physical pain. I had a stress fracture in my back thanks to playing the entire season while injured. The doctors had considered surgery, but I opted to wear a hard-back brace that went from my shoulder blades to my sternum. My body hurt, and my pride hurt. I felt burdened and frustrated.

On the positive side, I was free from drugs and gambling. The Greek government has zero tolerance of drug use, and I would be deported immediately if caught. And because they had seen the ravaging effects of gambling, you had to show proof of funds to even enter a casino. I tried to get in twice and was denied — thank God.

Even through I wasn't using drugs or gambling, things weren't perfect. My body was a mess and so was my mind. Fear and worry clawed at me constantly. I felt like I had to worry and keep finding reasons to do so. Was my back ever going to heal? Was I going completely bald? Did my girlfriend plan to leave me? Had I done permanent damage to myself with football and drug use?

These and many, many more questions kept cycling through my head, hounding me every day. The only relief I found came when I took walks through Plaka, the ancient section of Greece. It was there, on the cobbled marble stone streets, passing the tiny shops, in the place where my people walked for thousands of years, that I felt some solace.

One day, while walking home from work, I looked up and saw the ancient Acropolis bathed in the fading sun's brilliant glow. It was so beautiful! And it stood the test of time. Maybe I could too.

The problem was, I felt totally alone. When I first came to Greece, I was surrounded by cousins and friends my age, but they had since returned to their jobs and schools throughout Europe. My father had warned me this would happen.

"All of your friends are going to leave. You are going to be stuck around a bunch of old people with nothing to do and no one to talk to. You'll be bored out of your mind, Gregory."

His final words were like the last temptation at the cross. "Stay a little while longer, then let me get you a ticket to come home."

He was right. I'd been so headstrong and sure that Greece was the answer to my problems. But now I was there with absolutely no plan. I also had no ability to communicate. No one spoke English except my 65-year-old aunt Corinna, a psychology professor who worked in Crete during the week. I would be living with her for the first few months.

Corinna was also my godmother. She loved me like I was her own son. She made all my meals, like fresh-chopped salads, fried potatoes, and small steaks or pork chops. She also listened to my concerns.

"Why does Taki drink so much?" I complained. "It makes it hard to get him down the stairs. And Roula takes the longest, but she insists on leaving first."

My aunt was sitting on the one chair in her apartment, reading the newspaper while watching her ancient television set.

"I am surprised Taki and Roula even come," she replied without looking at me. "They have not spoken to each other in years."

"Really, why?" I asked.

"It's not worth getting into. They just don't talk anymore, that's all," she replied, still looking at her newspaper.

"So, then why are they coming?" I felt genuinely confused.

She looked up from her newspaper. "They are coming for you," she said before returning to her reading.

They were coming *for me*. They put their differences aside for me. I felt like a total asshole.

After that day, I began to push my boulder up the hill, not as a curse, but as a personal mission. I took this guiding task as my own.

In the middle of a flight of stairs, there was a window which the carpenter installed the wrong way so that it opened into the stairwell. I took great pride in remembering to close that window before anyone arrived and knocked their head.

These old people took so long on the stairs, moving step by step, that I began to notice the expressions on their faces, the unusual cracks in the wall. Each ascent would take a good five to ten minutes, so I had no choice but to pay attention to the view. By doing so, I felt myself slowing down.

Costa leaned against me as the staircase curved, and I steadied him. Doing so gave me a sense of honor and accomplishment. I began to feel needed and I had to go at his pace, not mine. Finally, I started thinking of someone other than myself.

But not having anyone to talk to wore me down. I could handle the slow walk up and down the staircase, but not being able to talk to anyone was like riding an elevator with a stranger, both of us looking awkwardly at the slow dial as floors passed.

I used to go to the village and try to order my lunch in Greek. The restaurant owners would either laugh or look confused at my attempts, while the people behind me stood impatiently as I stammered out my order.

One day, I burst out to my aunt, "I can't take it anymore! I can't understand a word anyone is saying to me. Everyone is making fun of me right to my face! I just can't learn this damn language!"

Aunt Corinna let me vent out my frustration.

After I was done, she said, "Gregory, I couldn't understand anything when I first came to America. Nothing. And then, one day, I just started to speak. That is what is going to happen to you too. One day, you will break through and be singing like a bird in Greek."

Her words gave me hope, and I continued my feverish study of Greek. Every day on the bus to work, I brought a list of twenty or thirty words to memorize. I even bought a bunch of children's books from the corner store to help me. One of them was about this new structure called the European Union, each of the different countries represented by animals. I read it constantly, each time learning a new word or phrase.

One day, I was with a group of people at a coffee shop. Someone said something, and I put together a sentence or two in response. The guy answered back, and I responded again. Then I stopped, shocked.

I looked around to make sure those replies came from me. They had, and the looks on my companions' faces confirmed it. I spoke Greek! It felt like a fresh river running through my mind and heart. It happened just like Corinna said it would.

At the end of my seven-month stay in Greece, I had accomplished two things: I learned Greek and I ferried old people up and down stairs. But these small acts turned out to have great power.

Chapter 18

Hungry for Hunger

Greece had given me a leg up. I cleaned up my act and moved from Greece to Arizona, far away from the influence of my former life. I talked my way into a top university and made it onto their football team. I was so excited and felt as if I had a new lease on life. I'd been drug-free for almost a year. I was in college, working, and playing football. I was really living. The days at my former college seemed like distant memories, as if they had nothing to do with me.

One day, while walking back from school, I entered a pizzeria just across from my apartment. The worker there was young and had a big, winning smile. He was wearing a Yankees cap. When people from the East Coast meet in Arizona, they form an immediate bond. Naturally, I asked him if he was from New York.

"No, but the owner is," he replied.

We had a great conversation, and I eventually came back and met the owner and the other guys who worked there. At first, I would occasionally stop in for a slice of pizza. Then I started spending more time hanging around the pizzeria, and eventually I started working there. The other workers smoked a lot of weed. So I got back into that. But I still had a lot of good things going; football and school acted as buffers between me and my old, bad habits. Like the saying goes, it was "just weed."

I discovered that many people living in Arizona who came from the East Coast were relocated by the law and were former criminals. Most of the people I met had spent many years in prison. I became accustomed to having violence around me and even began breaking the law myself. I started to re-enter the dark underworld and kept going deeper and deeper. It started off with two or three people, then I'd meet another two or three individuals worse off than them. There were these concentric circles of darkness that kept rippling out farther.

Somewhere in the midst of this decline, I developed knee problems. After the football season, I got a small surgery and was put on morphine. I loved the feeling of being on morphine. It was like time traveling to a point in my life where I felt pure joy, ecstasy, and just so good in my body.

Before I went to Greece, I'd been abusing painkillers. When I got home from the operation, I was still in a euphoric state. As I came off the morphine, I really wanted to get high. The doctor gave me a prescription that was supposed to last me a week. I finished it in one day, trying to recreate that feeling of total bliss morphine had provided me. As that effect wore off, a fierce throbbing pain ripped through my stomach, and I had to call the doctor.

"Doctor, I'm having horrible pains in my abdomen. Like the grim reaper is taking his sickle and ripping up my stomach."

He was worried. "I need you to come back immediately to the hospital." He was going to run tests to make sure an infection hadn't developed.

When I got there, he asked me if I had been taking the medication he gave for the pain.

For a second, I thought about lying but instead admitted the truth.

"I finished it."

He looked at me with a quizzical expression. "Why in the world would you do that?

I thought: Why in the world wouldn't I?

I spent an entire day at the hospital, going through a battery of tests and drinking charcoal to see if I was infected. I wasn't infected. I was in withdrawal. Right afterward, I started using opiates. After that, I turned my body into a garbage can that I filled with alcohol, weed, pills, hallucinogens, and whatever else was available.

You know what happens when the same man travels down a different road? Unless he really changes, he just repeats his journey. The road changes, but the road runner remains the same.

The Greece Effect had officially worn off. I ended up back where I'd been and far worse. To top things off, I was immobile and on crutches. The gambling problem had returned with a vengeance, and it seemed I had just traded Atlantic City for Las Vegas. Now, I was back to doing everything that I'd been doing in my last college.

I thought back to myself in Greece, working, living clean, learning to slow down, surrounded by family and friends, speaking a language fluently, a language I had taught myself. From that position of strength, I had gone back to the States and had only grown stronger. I'd built myself up. And after that, I'd toppled. What's incredible is that I didn't even really realize it.

I was a wreck when I came back home during a semester break. All I wanted to do was hide in my room, watch television, and brood about my life. The last thing I wanted to do was to see anyone who knew me, especially from high school because it would confirm how bad I'd become.

I could just picture it. I would ask them questions about how and what they are doing, and they would reel off where they were graduating from college, where they got their job, and oh by the way, who they were dating now. So, no thanks, I didn't want to see anyone.

But I couldn't stay locked up forever. One night I went to the YMCA — I always chose hours when I thought I wouldn't be seen. At the basketball court, I noticed a tall, lanky guy shooting baskets. I thought I recognized him. Tim!

I was actually okay with bumping into Tim. He was a good guy, and yet you could sense he had no real confidence in himself. He was not what you'd call super manly or popular. I liked him a lot — he was funny and smart — but some part of me didn't respect him because he was a pushover. I treated him like a sidekick, because I could.

He still had the same perfectly groomed hair like Clark Kent. Same clothing style too. As we started to talk, I could tell something was up. Something had changed. He held himself differently. Sturdier, somehow. He seemed self-contained. I tried to subtly compete with him by name dropping some cool places I had been, and some of the football players I played against who were now in the NFL. Basically, I was trying to assert my superiority, and to knock him back into his low-man-on-the-totem-pole place. But Tim was completely unfazed. He deflected me by not deflecting me at all! He radiated ease.

That really bugged me. He was supposed to be the inferior one, who by comparison would make me feel taller, more put-together. We met and spoke a few times after that. Each time, I noticed this subtly yet significantly altered Tim, and it made me envious and annoyed.

My curiosity won, and I asked him what had happened. He gave me some evasive answer. Finally, I demanded he tell me what had brought about this change. He said he'd stumbled upon some books that contained a lot of amazing ideas. He'd spent the last year and a half trying to put them into practice. You could call it a spiritual path.

Huh? I knew some of those books. I'd even picked one up and had thumbed through a few times, thought it had some cool spiritual ideas. Then I forgot about it and flung the book aside. But Tim, he had run with it.

After spending some time with him, I could see how deeply he had incorporated the books' messages. It made me so angry that he had this power and discipline to him, maybe even glimmers of greatness. I irrationally felt as if he'd stolen something from me. That greatness could've been mine if I had taken those books half as seriously as Tim. He'd seen what I couldn't. He found his self-worth, he found a spiritual path inspired by a series of books. And I was sinking. It was a total reversal.

I spent most of my semester break with him. Tim had no interest in converting me because there was nothing to convert me to — the books just contained ideas and practices. Still, he let me hang around. It was clear the books were the yeast in his life, what made him rise and keep rising. He was not a lanky, uncoordinated, pushover anymore. I wanted some of that energy too. I told him that I was going to go to Mexico to take psychedelics to "find myself."

He listened carefully and then told me: "I would never do that."

"Why not?" I asked.

"I would never do harm to my body. It's my physical vehicle in this lifetime."

Well, that was it. That statement not only inspired me to commit to total sobriety, but it also convinced me that I needed to know what Tim was doing to achieve this spiritual ease. I was hooked. Tim and I spoke for hours each day over the phone after I went back to Arizona. During those conversations, he shared with me what he knew.

The main focus was on a deep attitude shift. First, anything you do, you do it with total commitment, giving your absolute best, as though it were your final act on earth. When you cook your dinner, you treat a piece of fish as though it were sacred. That was how Tim handled all food. Even tying his shoelaces was imbued with deep respect.

Seem steep? That was just the beginning. Next, Tim said that your life is 100% your responsibility. Absolutely NO self-pity, no blaming others. Everything in life is high stakes.

Well, this philosophy made total sense to me. I was used to the idea of fighting for my life. In football, you are always acutely aware that everyone on the other team is out to hurt you. You don't get angry at that. You accept it. And you use that stark reality to motivate you.

This new philosophy was like being told something I'd sensed all my life. I started rigorously applying these practices in my life. I became more disciplined than when I'd trained for my football comeback. The sense of mission I felt made all the difference. Life was not about what happens in the physical world, and what you gain materially, or who you are socially, because all of that — all of it — disappears the moment you die. The real worth of life, the salt of life, was in the unseen: the spiritual, energetic world. That world became the blood running through my veins, the oxygen getting pumped into me, that made me eager to get up each morning. Tim activated my spirit. He made me hungry for something I never knew I was hungry for: inner spiritual greatness.

The names of these books and what happened to Tim and to us was so massive that I cannot go into it right now. At another time I hope to share more about the books and what happened to me. For now, what is important is that Tim had activated my hunger. The seed of hunger had been planted.

* * *

I wish I could say I found my path and rode off into the sunset, achieving flawless victory. But that's not what happened. I got derailed. I fell, hard. This time it was not due to drugs. No gambling, no women, no bad friends. Nothing. Perhaps it was as simple as the myth of Icarus: I flew too close to the sun. But when I fell, I fell so hard that all of my gains were wiped out.

So there I was. I had done my best, I had found the spiritual way of life. I had surrendered to it and practiced it diligently. I had thrown myself completely into the spiritual way of life, and I still failed.

The hardest part was the longing, the deep desire to be on the spiritual path as I once was. But this path claims you even more than you can claim it. It's not something you can dictate when to pick up and put down. The fact that I couldn't figure out why I failed was eating away at me. Who was to blame for this?

I blamed myself. If the body is a temple, I had destroyed it again and again, along with my mind. I couldn't save myself. My life was spiraling out of control. I needed to be rescued from myself. But there would be no Greece this time. I had no place to go. So I went home.

Chapter 19

One Year to Live

I was living back in New Jersey with my parents. I wasn't working. I couldn't get a job. I barely even left the house. I didn't have any friends. I stopped talking to people; forget about girlfriends. I was still good-looking, but anyone who saw me picked up immediately that it was better to stay away.

Each day I had to try to find something to do, some way to pass the time. The biggest event on my daily agenda was going out for coffee. But I knew what I absolutely didn't want to do: be around people.

My father had retired, so being at home would prompt the usual questions: What are you going to do today? How are you feeling? Are any of your friends home?

Those question felt like pouring acid on a wound. So, I'd go out to find solace and escape these questions.

One day I couldn't bear the idea of talking to anyone, not even the the cashier at the coffee shop. So I went to the town library instead. As I sat there at a desk in a corner, I felt a surge of fury rise in me. The reality of my life started to set in. It wasn't supposed to be like this.

Before, I had been a big worrier. Worry meant I thought my life wasn't on track. Worry meant my life was precious to me. Now, it no longer was. When you care about your car, you take care of it, make sure it's getting what it needs. If you don't care, you're okay with it breaking down. Instead of worry, I raged.

I will drive this car into a wall, I told myself.

I looked around me at the library. I remembered that years ago, the town was thinking of tearing down the library because nobody used it.

That's what needs to happen, I thought. But not to this building: I need to destroy myself.

Then I remembered that someone realized the library wasn't being used because it was outdated, not because it was irrelevant. This person convinced the town to modernize the library, to reconstruct it, make it more accessible and even make additions. One of the additions was a sweeping panoramic reading room where the morning light cascaded in. Now the town's readers, mostly old men like my father, went there to read the newspapers for free. So, instead of destroying the library, the town saved it.

The thought of being saved angered me. I didn't deserve to be saved.

I got up and left the library. I walked outside to the courtyard and sat on a bench. I looked to the field across from where I was. It was Memorial Field, where I used to play as a child.

I saw the town pool that we used to call the "park puddle." I learned to swim there. I remember my mother sitting at the side of the pool, clapping with joy and pride, a huge smile on her face while I took my first strokes, arms swinging, my face a mixture of determination and joy. I knew I was loved. I knew I was safe. I knew I would make it.

But I didn't make it. I ended up here. Again. What did I do to end up back here? Across from me stood a statue of a little girl, smiling ear to ear, playing with a hula hoop. I thought of my own lost happiness, and her face disgusted me.

I had gone so far. But I fell, and now I couldn't get anywhere, and never would. I had no friends, no job, no nothing. As for family, who cares about your family? I felt the rage building and building like a volcano about to blow. How could this have happened? How could I have screwed up like this?

My energy was so toxic, I knew I could hurt myself with it. I felt myself on the verge of something bad. As my frustration and rage grew, I started to feel like the only way to control it was to turn it against myself. I felt unable to stop. I was now talking loudly, almost yelling at myself.

"You idiot! You fool! You fuck-up!"

If someone sober and sane had walked by, they would've seen someone screaming at himself and called the police.

I felt like I was both pushing myself and being summoned toward the edge of the cliff by some unknown force that wanted to hurt me. I was like a helpless man being held at the nape of my neck, being led to the gallows by an executioner.

As I was dragged by this executioner, I heard some angry judge inside me delivering the verdict.

Guilty of being a bad brother!

Guilty of irreparably destroying your body with football and drug use!

Guilty of taking every opportunity and squandering it!

Guilty of wasting your parent's money!

Guilty of not finding a job!

Guilty of being back here . . . again.

The judge was right on all counts. I couldn't argue

with him. I felt compelled to let the executioner finish the job. I felt it and pushed towards that final destination.

As the rage grew and the end was near, another voice inside me said softly, "This is the gate of no return. If you harm yourself, there will be no coming back."

This realization provoked something within me, and I paused. I took a sweeping look at the field: the grass, the trees, the statue, the baseball diamond. Memories of my childhood played out before me. I saw joy. I saw wonder. I saw hope. I saw a child — a child worthy of love, worthy of life.

I lowered my head and sank into a long moment of silence.

"One more year!" I blurted out.

That statement came so definitively that I wondered if it came from me or through me.

"What was that?" the executioner hissed.

Even though I didn't totally know what I meant, I repeated: "One more year."

"One more year for what?"

"Give me one more year . . . to rebuild my life."

"You've done that — many times. And yet here you are. You always end up here. Look at yourself now. Look at who you've become. You cannot come back from this. You have failed."

Those words felt final, and I knew that it was true. I then voiced something I had never been able to say before.

"*I know that. I know that I've failed.* I don't totally understand how I got here, but I'm not going to resist it anymore. I accept that. I know how bad things are, but I just want to appreciate my life for one year. Give me one year. I want to care about my life. I will put everything I have into this year — everything."

"You are postponing."

"No! In one year I'll come back here and I will face my fate. If I make no progress, I will go without fighting. If my best isn't enough, I will accept that it's over. Give me one more shot. It will be my best shot."

I kept repeating the phrase, "I will appreciate it, I will appreciate it. One more year . . ."

I was still talking to myself, muttering my prayer over and over again, when I slowly opened my eyes.

I stood facing the windows of the sun-bathed room of the library. The old men were still there, quietly reading their newspapers. The statue of the hula-hooping girl still stood frozen, smiling in front of me. The scene was exactly the same. But something had changed.

I didn't even have to look around. I already knew. The executioner had left. I had been granted my one year.

Chapter 20

The Eagle Has Landed

I had made the decision to live, for one year. I would do whatever I had to do to pull myself out of the swamp. I would take the steps.

The first thing I had to do was get a job. I labored over *The Star-Ledger, The New York Times,* and whatever job website I could, looking for The Job. I had no idea where to begin. Most of the jobs asked for experience or specific training; they seemed way beyond me.

One day, I came across a job at Princeton University that needed an assistant to the chair of the neuroscience department. Even though I had no qualifications, I applied. For some reason, I was called back and brought in for an interview. It was one of my first real interviews. A moment of excitement! There was hope. I was thrilled. I casually told my family as if it were no big deal.

It was a younger woman who interviewed me. She explained how the department chair was really busy and needed someone to keep track of all his scheduling, book his travel, his appointments. It was a very demanding job.

The interviewer turned to me and asked, "Do you think you would like this job?"

It was clear to me that I would absolutely hate this job. Here I was, this big jock football player, following around some professor maintaining his schedule. No way! But I formulated my best bullshit response. I assured her that I would love the job and was very organized.

She looked at me carefully and confessed that she had her doubts. I appreciated that. In most of these interviews, you have no idea what they're thinking. But I felt, "Oh please, please don't realize the truth. Please don't realize I'm not a good fit. You have the power to take away years of suffering, both before and after this moment. Please just take away my pain."

"It's a demanding job," she repeated. "I just don't know if you'll like it or if you have the experience."

By the time I left, I knew the job wasn't mine. But I also understood what had actually brought me to this interview in the first place. I was hoping I would schmooze my way into Princeton. I wasn't there to get this job at Princeton. No. What I wanted was to get into Princeton, but I didn't want to do all the work to actually get in. I was trying for one Hail Mary pass to get my life together. And I wanted to be able to say, I work at Princeton.

As I left, even though I was disappointed, I felt a sense of relief come over me. There would be no quick fix. I was going to have to do the slow, steady, hard work to make progress in life. Freedom would not be free.

One day, while walking through town, I spontaneously walked into the town bakery and coffee shop, Cafe Beethoven. I went to the back and greeted a man and a woman. They were both dressed casually, but the man was behind the counter so I figured he worked there.

I mustered up the courage to ask if they were hiring. We got into a basic discussion of who I was, what hours I was looking for, my experience. They both looked curious and engaged. The man, who turned out to be the owner, said to me: "I like your energy. You're hired."

Wow! Somebody actually wants me. Finally some progress, I thought.

The first day at the job, the owner walked me around the store, giving me a brief overview. Then he introduced me to a frizzy, long-haired kid. I shook his hand and said hello.

"This is Teddy," the owner said. "He's going to be your shift manager."

I looked back at the owner like, you've got to be

kidding me. This kid looks 14 years old! I later found out he was 16. I was 26 at the time. I got over it. What the hell. How bad could it be?

The day started out pretty normal. I took some coffee orders. I folded cake boxes. I was feeling like I was doing okay, getting in the groove of things. But pretty soon, Teddy was making comments about my work.

"We don't do it this way." "When you take an order, write is down as they tell it to you." "Write more clearly." "Bring out all the drinks at the same time." "Cut the cake like this, not like that."

It's not that he did anything unusual or wrong, but each time he corrected me, I felt bossed around, and it was a massive blow to my pride. Here I was, this 26-year-old, with a bachelor's degree, a former Division 1 football player, and this little kid that looked like Bob Ross was telling me what to do. It was ridiculous. After a few weeks of this, I started to doubt that I had made the right decision to work there.

Still, I showed up. And it turned out that I was doing a pretty good job. I was particularly good at cleaning the restaurant. I would meticulously sweep and mop every night, cleaning every corner of the building. I also learned how to make espresso drinks. I would carefully measure the exact weight of the expresso, then pack it in really tightly so the espresso gets extracted when it comes through. The key to making the crema is to steam it in such a way to get a perfect blend of foam and milk. It creates a velvety texture. That's what makes those drinks so delicious.

One time, a group of people were visiting from Italy. I served them at their table. A middle-aged woman, beautifully dressed, took a sip and then raised her eyebrows and looked at me with a smile. "Very nice," she said. I felt so honored that I had just impressed an Italian woman with my cappuccino.

I started to relax into the job and feel a sense of accomplishment, but pretty soon another old dynamic of mine reared its ugly head. Teddy was giving me basic directions. But for everything he told me, I had an answer. Simple things, like before cutting the cake run the knife under hot water. It makes sense, but to me at the time, I wanted to argue, so I said, "What's the point? I can cut the cake perfectly without a hot knife."

It wasn't only with this young kid that I had trouble taking direction. A long-standing issue of mine with male leaders was to compete with them. I would take the job and then act like an asshole. In my mind, I was demonstrating my superiority. In relationships with men, I chose to become competitive in order to prove my worth.

Once I had worked for an Italian restaurant in Arizona. I heard that this guy whose family was very famous in town decided to open his own high-class restaurant. I had very little experience but somehow talked my way into this job. He gave me a chance and hired me, but it was downhill from there. I was such a wiseass. I would get into arguments with the other workers, teasing them about random things. It got so bad that one night, me and the owner almost got into a physical fight in the kitchen.

Shortly after that, I started looking for a new job. I remember waking one morning and reading the newspaper. As I read through one ad, I recognized the description. It was my job! I called the owner anonymously, pretended to be asking for the job and then sprung it on him.

"So, when were you going to tell me I was out of a job," I said while I thought 'Gotcha!'

He stuttered momentarily, paused, and then calmly leveled with me. "Listen. You came in and talked a good game. But you're not delivering and you're not pleasant to be around. You are not doing a good job."

There was no anger in his words. I didn't even respond. He was right.

And now, at Cafe Beethoven, I felt compelled to repeat my competition with men. But the café owner was more secure in himself and just had no personal incentive to compete with me. That, along with the genuine respect he had for me, earned my respect. I worked very hard for the boss.

My shift started around 5 p.m. and ended at 10 p.m. Each night at the bakery, I'd look out the window and stare at a streetlamp, wondering what direction my life would go, what the future held for me.

As I walked home at night, the streets were quiet; there were only ever a few cars out at that time. There was something extremely powerful about walking home in the darkness, when no one was awake. I could hear my own longing, my own yearning, my own feelings. The power of the night was also reminding me that this was a story whose ending was veiled in its darkness.

That excited me — I was starting to wonder how the story would unfold, even believing again that it might have a happy ending. I would hear a voice inside saying, you're doing it, you're showing up, you're making progress. Keep going.

As I made the slow walk home, past the library and through the dark and silent streets, I sensed the truth. The town was sleeping, but I was waking up.

After about a year of working at the cafe, I told my parents I was going to quit to move onto something bigger and better. My father was supportive, but my mother thought otherwise.

"It just doesn't feel that you are done there yet," she said.

I didn't understand. What more was there to be accomplished or learn at Cafe Beethoven? But her words made me reflect. I was always jumping into the next job, the next town, the next opportunity, the next activity. I never stayed anywhere long enough to ground myself, establish roots, and grow.

As a kid, I used to sit by the sea and watch the Greek fisherman bringing their daily haul of octopuses back. They had an unusual way of tenderizing these creatures. For hours they would sit and pound each octopus against the rocks on the shore as the meat became softer.

I decided to stay at the bakery for another year. I stayed, allowing the process to work on me, tenderize me like an octopus, over and over, day after day. In the end, it took two years to beat some of my bad habits — and to beat the asshole — out of myself. I flushed out my desire to compete with male leaders instead of taking direction. I chiseled away at my pride. Instead, I was allowing myself to join life on its terms, moving at its pace. I was finally allowing myself to feel grounded. I was landing.

Chapter 21

Learning to Love

My town's culture emphasized progress and advancing. Everyone my age was off pursuing their advanced degrees or working in Manhattan. So there were no other guys for me to hang out with. Nobody.

Not that I would have been interested in hanging out with anyone. I tried my best to avoid people as I went to and from Cafe Beethoven. When strangers met me, I could feel them evaluating me, judging, and coming to conclusions about me. They sensed something was deeply wrong with me. It's easy to spot someone who isn't thriving.

Worst of all was meeting people who knew me from years ago, when I was healthy, strong, and confident. When I had promise. Once, I ran into my best friend from childhood. He said, "I remember us playing, and just always knew by the way you competed that there was something unique about you, that you were special and would make something big out of yourself."

Yes, I had made something big. I'd made a big mess, and it was hard to see the disappointment on his face. The big unspoken question was, "What are you doing home?" It was unheard of for someone my age to be living at home. I was the poster child for what is now a national syndrome: young men living with their parents until they're 30 years old and even past that.

My hometown was a neighborhood-centric community. People were friendly and talked to each other. Next door to me lived a young Greek couple who formed a connection with my parents. I eventually met them but had not yet personally met their kids.

When I was walking to and from work, I'd pass their house and often see a young boy of about three or four standing at the glass front door looking out. He had dark brown hair and glasses so thick that it made his eyes look like two round circles. One thing I noticed was his constant expression of joy. He was smiling, and his eyes, magnified by his glasses, were perpetually wide open with wonder. Something about his look gave me a feeling of glee.

One day, on my way back from Cafe Beethoven, his mother came out and said, "Would you mind making some time to play with LJ? He said you told him that you'd play with him."

It's true. I probably had promised to play with him.

And now I was being called on it. I felt burdened. I couldn't say no because I knew even if I lied that day, I couldn't lie for the next day, and the day after.

The next day, I walked into his backyard. It had a large swing set, a basketball hoop attached to the garage, and a well-maintained green yard. We played tag, then sat on the swings, then played baseball and basketball. One tree was first base, the other tree was second base, the wood chips were third. I remember picking him up so he could reach the hoop in the basket, and when he made a basket, I would jump for joy along with him.

When I came home, I told my mother about my playdate with LJ.

She said, "Oh, he is adorable. And Karen and Jimmy are doing such a great job getting him services."

"What do you mean?" I asked.

"LJ has Down syndrome," my mother said.

I didn't believe it. He seemed to be just a regular, happy kid, only happier. I challenged my mother, telling her that she was wrong. "LJ is perfectly normal," I scoffed.

The whole idea of Down syndrome or any limitation — physical or mental — had always made me uncomfortable, if not judgmental. Even my father, who has a rare skin condition called vitiligo, was a source of embarrassment for me as a child.

I began playing with LJ practically every day. He would be sitting behind the glass front door, waiting for me. When I passed by, he'd open the door or shout through the window, "Gee-gree! Hi Geegree!" I loved hearing him call my name. His genuine energy and enthusiasm for seeing me, over and over again, started to break through my wall. You would think I was a bright-red fire engine or some iconic train passing by. He loved seeing me. Bit by bit, some of his love began to seep into me.

At that time, I still refused to accept that he was in any way different or limited. I just felt no judgment from LJ. It didn't matter if I limped around because my body hurt, or my hair was a mess, or I was going nowhere in my life. I saw that LJ didn't, or couldn't, judge me. He was incapable of it. And that liberated me.

Despite the progress I had made in sticking with one job, I still felt caught up in shame and defeat. This was most apparent in my interactions with people and with the world.

At Cafe Beethoven, I had to relate to customers, asking for their order, taking the food and drinks to their table. "What cake do you want?" This level of basic, short interaction was doable for me. But I struggled with deeper connections.

One time, a gorgeous Indian woman came into the store. She boldly told me she liked me and asked me out on a date. She was studying to become a doctor. I was embarrassed that I had nothing going on in my life, so I made up an excuse that day and never followed up. I simply could not connect at a deeper level. I was really closed off.

But now, somewhere in the midst of all this playing with LJ — tag, basketball, wrestling, running around in the backyard — I lost myself. I started to feel more open and giving.

There was an experiment where a group of old men were taken to the mountains and told to simply act like they were decades younger. After five days of reading, talking, and playing like they were when they were younger, these men experienced definite changes all over their body: their posture improved, blood pressure decreased, positive neurotransmitters increased. At the end of a week, these old men were playing tag football! In this way, acting like a kid can resurrect parts of that inner child.

With LJ, I could be whoever I really was, moment to moment, and give our interactions my all. I found, after playing with LJ for an hour or two, I wasn't as judgmental of other people, and I could deflect any judgment I felt coming toward me.

My connection with LJ lasted as long as I was home, about three years. Our interactions profoundly changed the way I connected with people. I could finally see that there was a way of living from a place of total freedom, to give and receive without judgment or reservation.

I thought of the Executioner and the Judge, and how I had made my journey a comeback story. I was appreciating my life. I had even completed my Master's degree in Psychology. I got a job in my field. My life was opening up to me.

Still, living at home was never easy. The urge to grow and be free always nagged at me. I was getting frustrated and restless. I made up my mind to move out.

I wasn't moving out because I hated my dad who was forever falling asleep snoring on the couch at 7 p.m., nor because my mom was nagging me constantly about what I was going to do with my life. I was moving out because, for the first time in my life, I had earned enough money to live on my own. So I started my apartment search.

* * *

As I walked around an apartment I'd seen advertised, nearly everything was great, especially the low rent. But there was one thing: this place was shared by three other college students.

I thought, "I'm 29 years old. I can't live with a bunch of 21-year-old students. This is ridiculous."

Still, I looked at the room that would be available to rent. I was really attracted to that room. My uncle who is a fisherman in Greece taught me that when you see a group of rocks that are very clean in the ocean, you know there's an octopus home underneath, because they clean their home so thoroughly.

When I saw the room I'd be renting, it had been meticulously cleaned, like an octopus lived there. The shoes were in a row outside the room, not inside. Everything inside was organized. The space was perfectly utilized. It left a strange and beautiful impression on me. When I came back the next day, still trying to decide whether to take the room, I met the person whose room it was. I met the Octopus.

Her name was Satomi, and she was a student from Japan. As we spoke in the kitchen, I felt the rest of the room recede. It was just me and Satomi. Even the other young woman, who was in the room, almost vanished. I decided right there to take the room.

It was June. Because this was essentially a college dorm, all the college renters left at the start of summer to go home. That meant I was alone. One of the first nights I stayed there, I heard a loud voice laughing and talking on the phone in one of the rooms. I wasn't alone. As fate would have it, one of the residents let Satomi live in their room while she looked for her next apartment.

During that first week, we'd eat dinner at the same time, and get into nice conversations. We eventually cooked a meal together. As a ritual, after dinner we would go for long walks. One weekend, I was going to the beach. I invited her, and she came. We'd gone out to dinner a couple of times, and to movies like *The Devil Wears Prada*, a movie I wouldn't normally see.

It was clear that she was special person. We had a very deep connection, but it wasn't lust or sexual chemistry. That was a challenge for me. I wanted lust to do the hard work for me. I didn't want to lift a finger. As a kid, my joy and outward energy was such that people naturally loved being around me. I became accustomed to receiving love and attention without actually doing anything to earn it. I was the boy who was loved too much. As this emotional entitlement grew, a form of passivity developed. I expected love, but couldn't create it.

And secretly, I was afraid of love. Because I was so averse to deeper intimacy, if I sensed that this relationship was going to lead to something deeper, I would've found a way to sabotage it. But because my connection to Satomi happened so innocently and quickly, I didn't even know it was happening.

We'd been dating a month — while living in the same apartment. Then she left when her new apartment in

New York became available. My ambivalence immediately kicked in because now more effort was required on my part. Did I really want to put energy into this woman who now lived in Queens? I was attracted to her, but I didn't feel lust, and if there was no lust, then what was the point? I wasn't a maniac in love. Hollywood led me to believe that's how it happens: You lose your mind completely and give up everything in the moment. It wasn't like that. It was a bond, something I'd never had any experience with at all. But then she left. For the first time, I had to call to make a date. Despite my inner back and forth, I asked her out.

We arranged to meet midway, at Bryant Park, and spend the day together. It was a Tuesday. We were on our cellphones trying to find each other. Finally, I saw her across the park. She was standing on the steps, her black straight hair grazing her shoulders, surrounded by the iconic London Plane trees. The sun filtered through the trees. She was wearing a lovely off-white shirt-sweater, and forest-green pants. I knew she was objectively attractive, but at that moment I was struck by her beauty. Her eyes were unique, full of depth and warmth.

We started to stroll around New York. At one point, she put her arm in mine. This feels so good, I thought. Still, I was waffling inside. Should we continue dating or stop seeing each other? It was getting in the way of us enjoying this gorgeous summer day. I stopped a Persian-looking man with a delivery van to ask directions to a particular restaurant. He told me, "You're not far," and then gave me directions. Then he looked at Satomi, back at me, nodded, and looked deep in my eyes. "Enjoy your company," he said.

This guy made it so simple. That was the moment I saw the date as an opportunity, a gift, rather than some puzzle I had to solve. His message was clear: Just enjoy your company and this magical day.

The rest of the day we spent in total bliss. We dined outside, and later sat on the green by the river and listened to beautiful, live jazz. We were walking back to our subway trains when spur of the moment, we went into a restaurant filled with hundreds of candles. It was the most healing sight. The place was packed, but they said we could sit at the bar if there was room. As I looked at the bar, there were two available seats, but in between those two seats sat a young couple, maybe in their 20s. I walked over to the bar and asked, "Could you please move over?" The woman gave me a funny look but moved over. She said to her boyfriend, "Our table will be ready in a minute, anyway."

As we sat down, Satomi asked me, "Do you know who that woman was who you asked to move?"

"No."

She told me it was a famous actress. I looked over and recognized her, but she looked normal, like a basic college girl. For me, Satomi's beauty radiated. I felt honored to be with her.

We ordered a few appetizers and had the best time in the contagious energy of New York. Afterward, we walked to the train station and said goodbye. It was a long day. I sunk back into the train seat and took a deep breath. A voice came into my head: "You will never be happier than you are with Satomi."

Sometimes, you're reading a book and not sure if it's going anywhere. You want to give up on it. Then you read the next page, and you see the author's gift, and you say, "You know what? I'm going to keep going. I'm going to read this."

I kept going.

Chapter 22

Meet My Mentor

At the end of my Master's Program in Psychology, I had an externship at Beth Israel Hospital in New York City. I started making a name for myself there. Staff would shadow me as I worked with clients. My supervisor said, "Gregory, you're showing us how this is done."

I'm really destined for this work, I thought, as I started to imagine my path to greatness.

After I graduated, I applied for hundreds of jobs all over the northeast and I finally got an offer. It was at a methadone clinic in Irvington, New Jersey, a notoriously rough area. I was so hungry for work that I took it right away, even though I knew it would be a very tough job. But there I went, walking through the ghetto in my dad's only designer blue blazer.

"Should I be worried?" I later asked a co-worker.

"No," he said, "Everyone in this area is going to think you're a cop."

Three weeks into my new job, my supervisor said I'd have to run a group for 75 to 100 people on Saturday, the day nobody wanted to come. But the attendees were court-ordered and came to get their methadone dose that would last the weekend. I'd spent the whole night preparing for my "debut." I was nervous and excited. I felt as ready as I could be, but when I arrived at the clinic the other counselor handed me a video.

"What's this?" I asked.

The counselor said, "The supervisor left a video for you to show."

My first thought was relief. I wouldn't have to face this intimidating crowd. But when I thought about playing the video, something didn't feel right. Screw it, I decided. I didn't want to rely on a video.

I introduced myself to the group. "Greetings, everybody. My name is Gregory." For some reason, I adopted a faintly British accent. "Obviously, I'm the new guy on the block."

The topic was our value system and how that relates to addiction and recovery. I asked questions and people answered. They were engaged, attentive. In short, I ran an exceptional group; it was a home run. I dropped the mic. I thought, "I'm going to be the best counselor on Earth."

The next time I ran the group, everyone was seated. When I walked in, they began applauding. I felt so validated. Yes! I had prepared well for this group too. But as I started running the group, I couldn't find my legs. I was trying to recreate the magic of that first experience. It's a horrible feeling to know as you're talking that you're bombing. And I did, big time.

A similar pattern was developing in my one-on-one sessions. The first session or two was powerful, intense, and edgy. But the follow-up was difficult. I kept trying to recreate the intense moment that happened in the first session. I wanted people to change in one moment. I didn't understand that change isn't always available right away.

I was a young, white counselor working with a primarily black crowd. They challenged me a lot in group. They told me I was young and didn't know shit. Even when they tried to let me help them, I had nothing to give. Nothing.

Jeremiah was another counselor at this clinic. He was very established and 50 years old to my 30. He was a massive, strong, charismatic guy — a preacher's son. We occupied two of the three basement offices, so I could hear his sessions when his office door was open. Generally, I tried not to listen, but his booming voice was so loud that it carried throughout the hallway.

"So, what are your goals with regards to your housing?" I heard Jeremiah ask a client in his deep, raspy voice. "Have you made any progress?"

There was nothing special about what he said, but the way he said it was very alluring to me. He had a slow, measured pace with a deep and lively voice. It was clear that he was really aware of what he was saying, that he was curious, listening, and taking what was said to heart. He made common life sound important and extraordinary.

He was not ordinary. You couldn't help but notice him. He dressed up like a 1950s gangster, his shirt untucked, his hair slicked back. He wore wing-tip shoes that made noise when he walked, so you could hear him from far away. He also smoked in his office, which was against the rules. He smoked in the bathroom too, the one set aside for the clients, and made himself comfortable there, relaxing and reading a newspaper while he puffed on one of his Newports. He had no shame about anything.

Every chance I got, I would observe him when he led a group. He sat perched on the very top of the chair, his feet on the seat. His groups were absolutely electric, profound, and funny. He knew how to provoke people, to irritate them — not in a malicious way but to engage them, to force them to look at their lives.

Once, he pulled me aside and explained his method.

"All I'm trying to do with these people is become the itch they have to scratch."

He knew that when people are comfortable, stuck, and in denial, it is because they don't want to face their life fully. But if you turn their life into a persistent itch, they have no choice but to scratch at it.

Jeremiah grew his eyebrows long, and he'd twirl them like a detective twirling his mustache. He looked to me then like an old crocodile, some prehistoric character that kept finding ways to survive, and enjoying the process.

Even though Jeremiah had a larger-than-life personality, he could scale it back when he wanted to, by just sitting and quietly observing. He knew how to tuck his face just under the water, and all you saw were his eyes and this crafty crocodile smirk. He had the knack of coming and going without leaving a trace.

One time, our staff was having one of its mandatory all-day training sessions. These were torture. We all were just sitting there, bored out of our minds. Jeremiah was sitting in the very back, with his crocodile smirk, more quiet than usual. An hour later, I looked over my shoulder — he was gone. The crocodile had gone under and swum away.

Jeremiah and I began spending so much time with each other, the staff jokingly referred to me as his son.

We would talk about work and about life. Being around him was like standing at the foot of an ancient canyon: its timelessness, power, and wisdom was undeniable, and it naturally forced self-reflection.

What made him so special was his mesmerizing way of engaging with life and his incredible sense of humor. He was always getting into trouble at work, with the staff. I loved that about him. He laughed his big, outrageous laugh, cackling at his own ploys.

Once, in a group session, he took a piece of chalk and made a dot in the middle of the blackboard. "The thing you guys need to realize," he said in his powerful, resonant voice, "is you are just a tiny insignificant dot in the universe." I remember feeling the beauty of being right-sized and ego-deflated.

Jeremiah knew how to deal with addicts. Addicts never do what they're supposed to do, but they always expect to get what they want, when they want it. They develop effective strategies to get what they want through temper tantrums, lying, manipulating, and threatening. All the other counselors were unable to enforce basic rules. But Jeremiah never gave them what they wanted. Everyone knew there would be consequences with him if they didn't follow the rules.

Still, he knew when to let go. Clients weren't allowed to go out the back door because it opened into a residential area. There were strict rules about it because the neighbors were always complaining to the police. Once, a woman was raising a total shitstorm about going out the back door because she needed to get somewhere fast. I was fighting her on this. It was escalating.

Jeremiah came to me afterward. He said, "Hey Greg, why did you handle it like that?"

Part of the reason was because I was trying to be like him. Firm. Hold the line.

I said instead, "Because it's the rules."

He just looked at me and slowly shook his head.

"Okay fine." I crossed my arms. "So how would you have dealt with it?

"Simple. I would've walked up to the back door and stood in front of it. 'Listen,' I'd tell her. 'You can leave out this door today, but it's against the rules and I don't want you to ask to do it again. Deal?' Sometimes, Greg, you gotta take the path of least resistance."

I loved these lessons even though they stung my pride and ego. He was showing me how to show an addict the way to agreement. He was saying, 'Both of us will get a voice in this.' At the same time, when he stood in front of the door, he was showing me how to claim my power — as he had.

He was by far the best counselor I ever met. Even so, before each of his groups I'd find him outside standing on the steps, smoking. He looked so confident, but he shocked me once by confessing he did that to calm himself before groups. He never rested on his laurels. Each time he ran a session, it was like the first time.

These lessons were not easy. Once, Jeremiah was standing in the back of the room, observing me run a group. The group wasn't engaging at all, and I had no clue what I was doing. I was tanking. He walked out after five minutes. Later, he came by my office and poked his head in.

"Your groups are so dry," he said matter-of-factly and then walked away.

No coddling, no advice, no encouragement. But it was the truth, and I needed to face that. If I was going to become great, I would need to do it using my own power, no one else's.

I was making progress, though. One time, a woman had a full-blown seizure in the hallway. I calmly dealt with her from start to finish. I surprised myself even.

Afterward, Jeremiah walked up to me and said, "Great job, Greg. You're learning. You couldn't have done that months ago."

His validation, because he didn't give it out for free, meant a lot.

I spent two and a half years working with Jeremiah. When we first met, I was still deeply wounded and self-obsessed. I needed a man who would not lie to me, would incessantly challenge me, but also empathize with me. I was in need of a mentor.

Chapter 23

Victory Begins in Defeat

Satomi and I met in June. That was the exact same time I started working my first job in the field, at the methadone clinic with Jeremiah.

One morning in March, Jeremiah and I were standing on the steps just outside the basement when I told him I was going to ask Satomi to marry me.

"You don't want to do that," he said nonchalantly.

I was taken aback. It had been a struggle to get myself ready to marry her, and I was secretly hoping for his blessing.

"Why not?" I said.

"You don't love her," he said without even looking at me.

I froze. Was he right? Finally, I fired back at him.

"That's not true!" I argued with him, telling him the reasons I loved her. I put up a fight.

"Good," he said unfazed. "I was just testing you."

*　*　*

I am at the wedding venue. It's chaotic — coordinating all the details, the flowers, the catering, the chairs, the music. Everyone wants to talk to me about something. I am feeling overwhelmed and anxious and tense. I can't even enjoy my own wedding. I can't feel love. I can't feel joy. Maybe Jeremiah was right. Maybe I don't love Satomi. But this train is moving so fast that before I even realize it, I am standing at the altar while music plays. I don't know what to do, where to put my hands, where to look. This is the first wedding I've ever been to, and it's my own.

My nerves, my desire to control everything, is all coming out. Holy shit. I'm staring at my feet, trying to focus. My two brothers are standing next to me. It is hot, and I am sweating. I glance up and see Jeremiah in the back row, his huge frame crowded onto a small folding chair, dressed impeccably in a tailored gray suit, his hair slicked back. I'm touched that he showed up.

The music plays, and here comes Satomi with her father. She looks beautiful, but the dress, the makeup, the ceremony, the venue, the flowers, none of it feels real. I can't feel. I am so caught up in myself that I cannot notice it.

A ray of salvation comes. A tiny figure is walking down the aisle with a pillow and rings. Its LJ! He's wearing a little suit and is grinning broadly. We'd stayed in each other's lives all these years. This little kid taught me how to love, but nothing helps me now.

I'm frozen as we exchange vows. What am I going to say? I had been going back and forth between two sets of vows I'd written to be followed by a poem. When it's my turn, I pull out the book and read the poem. I finish and put the ring on Satomi.

What did I just do?! I didn't even read the vows I wrote! I look out at the audience of people. I know I bombed. In the back row, I see Jeremiah, slouching, looking bored. Great! Another dry group I screwed up in front of my mentor.

At the meal, I feel like anything but a grateful, blessed husband. Around me, people are dancing like crazy to Zorba the Greek. I am sitting at the table, trying to hide my frustration and sense of defeat.

My father gets up to make a toast. First, he has everyone clink glasses. I only find out later that's a signal for me to kiss the bride — a signal I missed. Then he starts reminiscing about me when I was kid.

"Once," he says, "Gregory tried out for the basketball team and didn't make it. I still remember how upset he was. But what really moved me was how afterward I'd see him go out every day to practice. He would even shovel the snow where the basketball court was during the winter to make sure he could practice. He wouldn't give up. And eventually he made the team."

I began to remember that day, how the coach turned me down. My immediate reactions were embarrassment and shock. Eventually, those feelings gave way to resentment, fury, and finally became a fire, one that would motivate me to push myself, my body and mind until I finally won, until I attained success. In that moment, I saw it was that defeat, that rejection, that made me into the competitor I'd become. I always knew I was competitive, but not until that moment did I realize why.

I got it! I needed to fail today. I needed to. So that I could instill in myself the fire to succeed.

That's how it always works with me. Every success I ever had began in a defeat. It must be this way. In basketball, in marriage, in life. Seated at the reception, I feel like shouting it out.

My eyes seek out Jeremiah to tell him, but the old crocodile has slipped away. That's okay. A weight rolls off me. I unloosen my tie and move my neck this way and that. I'm starting to breathe again.

Satomi looks at me innocently, like "What's up? Is everything ok?"

I look at her — her deep eyes, her warm smile. I'm finally seeing the beauty of this sacred moment, of her, of us.

I nod and reach for her hand.

The feeling I had swimming in the pool as a child came back. I knew that, somehow, I was going to make it.

Chapter 24

The Man Watching

This was a special desert. Don't think sand and cactus only. Think mountains, evergreen trees, and a natural river flowing through the Aravaipa Canyon.

I was here on a group retreat. On the final day, the group leader arranged for the participants to take a solo ceremonial walk through nature. I began snaking through the canyon, enjoying the respite from the sun, which can be fierce even during March in Arizona.

I was musing about a nice conversation I'd had with the inn's owner, who generously allows people to host retreats on his personal land. "As long as I have the deed to this land, I will allow people to use it for good purposes. It is too sacred to keep to myself."

I loved that! That's what's missing in this world, I thought. People giving freely from the heart instead of holding and hoarding land they don't even use. That's what I had loved so much about Greece — how nobody hoarded, just shared what they had.

That thought of freely sharing, or giving, brought me back to my college buddy, the one who begged to go to Greece with me. I said no then. I couldn't. I was trying to save myself. Later, I heard he had gotten arrested for smuggling drugs across the Mexican border. He tried afterwards to put his life together. But sadly, he did not make it. He died at 36.

Who knows, I thought, what might have happened if he'd made it to Greece. He might have fallen in love there, with a girl, with the village, with the whole way of life. At the very least, it might've given him a fresh start — a chance.

I must have zoned out and stopped looking at my surroundings, because suddenly I stood before a huge canyon wall.

What? Where did this come from? It was about fifty or sixty feet wide and thirty feet high. It was a sheer wall, and it was in my way.

I was annoyed. I couldn't go forward, only back, retracing my steps where I had already gone. We only had a couple of hours for this ceremonial walk in nature, and I didn't want to waste it.

I looked for a while at the canyon wall. The rocks were large boulders, the size of small cars. Each one resembled a pillar of Stonehenge. They were separated from one other, and it looked like there were grooves where I could wedge my hands and feet. The trickle of water falling down the wall meant any climb, aside from being near impossible, would be slippery and treacherous.

And yet I couldn't shake the awe. It looked like something God fashioned, built to be climbed. And it was in my way. So I started to climb, almost without thinking. I heard a soft rustle and spotted another participant nearby, a gentle soul in his 60s. I paused, and wondered what was going through his mind. To even attempt this climb seemed show-offy and unrealistic.

I didn't want to show off, but I also didn't want to go back. Up I went. The next rock was a few feet above, and I found a crevice in the wall to plant one foot. Then I took a few more steps. Look, Greg, I told myself. You have no intention of climbing the rest of the wall. I was only about ten feet off the ground, and it would be easy to just go back down or even jump.

I paused and leaned my head into the rocky wall, breathing in the cold whisper of those old stones. When I lifted my head, I felt a desire to keep going. Somehow, another two steps up the wall just happened. I was panting from the exertion and paused again, leaning into the wall to feel it. I took two more steps. Suddenly, I realized that I was almost halfway up the wall!

I can still come down, I assured myself. But something was keeping me going.

Some lines from Rilke's poem, "The Man Watching," came to me in the dry wind:

". . . were we to let ourselves, the way things do,
be conquered thus by the great storm,
— we would become far-reaching and nameless."

I sensed the man below watching this all unfold. I could feel his presence and took comfort that he could at least inform the guides and my family if anything happened.

It was insane to keep climbing, but onward I went, prowling up this wall, until the voice said: Now you are at the point where descending will be more difficult than ascending. And almost before I could understand what I had done, I took two more steps. This time I didn't even dare look down. I was so high up this wall. But the voice simply said: There is only one way — up. You cannot go back down. There is no other option.

My heart was pounding like a drum. It beat so hard, trapped in my chest, and I started to fear my own heart's thumping. But being up there brought me a strange clarity. I thought of hearing my daughter's heart beat for the first time. There was no fear then, so why now? What is to fear about your own heart? Let it beat. The stronger and louder, the better.

I was so nervous that I leaned into the wall once more and just allowed myself to take in my heart beating.

Then I saw the crack in the canyon. My throat went dry as brick. In order to ascend, I'd have to leap several feet across a gap in the wall, to the other side. I assessed the jump from a few angles. It was doable, but there could be no reservations or doubts. I'd have to go all in, like that time in high school football when I got lower and ran through the gauntlet of players screaming.

Oh boy, Gregory, you really screwed this up. You did it again, got yourself into another mess. What are you gonna do now? The question reverberated in my being. Yes, what am I going to do now?

I wiped all these feelings and thoughts away and re-centered myself in the simple truth in that moment: I am just a man on a wall who must leap to the other side.

I took a deep breath, knowing that if I hesitated, doubted, held back, that it could be my last breath. At that moment, there was such a comfort in having my hands wedged in that wall, my feet underneath me. But I would have to leave that comfort and security.

I centered myself and then with my animal body, with all of me, I leaped. I felt my body in flight for an eternal moment, and then the next thing I knew I landed smack on my stomach on the other side. I laid there, scanning my body for injury, my breath heaving, panting.

I pulled myself to my feet. I was okay. I had made it!

I stood at the top of the wall. I hadn't even known what awaited me, but luckily for me, it was flat ground. I wouldn't need to descend.

There was a feeling of elation, of relief and joy. I had made it. As I looked back to the canyon I had just leaped across, the image of my old college buddy came again into my mind. I saw him on the other side. He was stuck too. His eyes were blank with fear. I wanted to reach across the canyon, to help him, to save him. I wanted to tell him, bro, I can do it now. I'm ready. Let's go to Greece! But I knew I couldn't reach across. He would also need to find it within himself to make the leap.

C'mon, man! You can do this. You have to find your strength to leap. Once you make it, I can help you.

I stretched out my arms as if I could reach out to all the men I ever knew and would ever know. We would leap across the abyss, we would do it together, and have the adventure of our lives. We'd conquer mountains. We'd link up our spirits with the souls of all the men who came before us, charging heart-strong into battle.

I glanced down and saw the man watching from below. He was smiling, celebrating with me, as though we had jumped together. He was right. We had.

Looking at the man watching, and then at the jump we had made, I thought of something my teacher told me many years ago.

"Gregory, you are at the point where you need to make the leap. And when you do, one of two things is going to happen. Either a bridge will appear, or you will spread your wings . . . and fly!"

Afterword

There once was a flock of birds
That didn't know how to fly.
And for years and years those birds would meet
Each week to discuss why.

Every Wednesday without fail,
They'd walk to meet their crew,
And squawk and sing 'bout how to fly,
Each one sharing what they knew.

Well, Charlie Bird was walking once,
while reading the morning news,
And a car was flying at him so fast
that he barely had time to choose!

Charlie clearly knew the stakes
And dug down real deep,
And finally found within himself
what it takes to make the leap.

With one great thrust,
he jumped into the crystal clear blue air.
And with wind rushing through his feathers,
he flew without a care!

Well, Charlie Bird,
you may have heard
that bird just earned his wings!
And he could hardly wait 'til next Wednesday,
To tell his friends these things.

He taught 'em all the secret tips,
he showed them what he'd done.
A little like this, a little like that,
and they flew high one by one.

They danced around,
I swear to God,
They soared about the sky!
And when they landed back on earth,
They each let out a sigh.

After the meeting, they walked home,
each one waving goodbye.
They skipped and whistled through the streets,
Smiling at passersby.

But sadly the birds never thought,
nor sought to clarify,
why they had chose to walk home,
When they finally knew how to fly.

Acknowledgments

There is an old saying: How long did it take for you to write this book? 4 years. And 40 years.

For over 40 years, so many people have supported, loved, and guided me as though my life was their own. You have poured out your own blood to help me, and I could not and would not have made it this far without you. Thank you from the bottom of my heart. Especially my mother, who endured and hoped and wished and yearned for my safe passage. I love you, Mom.

For the 4 years, I wish to express my gratitude to Maia Danziger, who believed in my vision and helped with developmental editing at the beginning, turning blank pages into something. To Natsuyo Lipschutz, who helped me gain clarity and verbalize the system I was using. To Dr. Michael Gurian, who advised, supported and nurtured me and this project in the middle stages, helping turn this into an actual book worth consideration. To Jon Gosch, for his careful editing, joining the project with commitment and passion, and who ultimately helped crack the code for the structure of the book. For the magnificent force called Ruchama King Feuerman, who journeyed alongside me through the Underworld, confronting wild beasts and angry gods, and who helped me find the story that set me free!

To the young men I have worked with, and to their families, for trusting an unproven path and following it with total conviction. I will always be in awe of your faith and your trust, and will cherish what we did together. Thank you all!

To Isamu and Maya — my pride and joy — thank you for giving me the space to work on this, and the reason to do it. I promised you it was a Good World — and it is!

And for my beautiful wife Satomi, who supported me throughout this journey and who, as only she could, found the simple words to keep me going when I felt I could not go on. I once told her that writing a book on my work with men, one which is based on intuition and feeling, was impossible. She listened and then replied, "That may be. But then everything you have accomplished will die with you." That was the fire that made me decide to see this book to the end. I could not let this gift go unrecognized.